INDIA OF OUR TIMES

INDIA OF OUR TIMES
An Experiment in Democracy

Harish Kapur

GYAN

India of Our Times : An Experiment in Democracy

Rs. 540

ISBN: 978-81-212-1065-2

Published in 2011 in India by
Gyan Publishing House
23, Main Ansari Road, Darya Ganj
New Delhi-110002
Phones : 23282060, 23261060
Fax : 011-23285914
E-mail: books@gyanbooks.com
Website: www.gyanbooks.com

Laser Type Setting by: Rudra Computer Graphics, Delhi
Printed at : Chawla Offset Printers, Delhi

To
Sunita
With Affectionate Love

Contents

Preface

My academic research, throughout my professional life, was devoted principally to the study of the foreign policy of variegated nations with different outlooks and different orientations—countries as diverse as the former Soviet Union, China, Taiwan, the European Union and India. However notwithstanding all the variegation that characterises these national actors, there does exist a broad homogeneous methodological framework that permits a discerning analysis that includes such factors as history, geography, geopolitics, environments (internal and external), ideological orientations and the personality factors.

The experience of such an historical analysis made it possible for me to comfortably and scientifically stretch out to other sectors of history

This is what I have done. I have authored this manuscript on the contemporary internal history of India— a history that deals in Part I with the formation of the British Empire until its disappearance after World War II. Part II covers contemporary India after the independence of the country with a focus on its political and economic system, and the different societal aspects that determine India, including the types of leadership it has projected.

The basic running theme of this book is the establishment of democratic institutions, and the ramifications they have had on the different aspects of contemporary Indian society.

This study does not claim to be a work of original scholarship, and still less a work of reference; nor is it meant for those who know India well. Basically, it is a simple and a straightforward book written for those who wish to know the basic history of India written by a person of Indian origin who had spent all his academic life in Europe, and who has some views that may not correspond with more traditional perceptions of Indian history.

The book is based on diverse documentation available in different archives, and on considerable interactive discussions that I have had with people who were in know of things in India as well as abroad.

For my last book on the "Foreign Policies of India's Prime Ministers," I had the marvellous experience of meeting a number of living prime ministers, including I.K.Gujral, Narasimha Rao, V.P. Singh, Chandra Shekhar, and many of the close advisers of Indira Gandhi, Jawaharlal Nehru, Morarji Desai, who were in the corridors of power. To all of them I am indeed very grateful for the general discussions I had with them, and the exposure I had to their views on the different aspects of Indian history.

If there is any particular person that should be mentioned, I would like to thank I.K. Gujral for the myriad discussions I have had with him on many subjects pertaining to India.

I must, however, underline the fact that I alone am responsible for the views expressed in this study.

Ravoire,
Switzerland

Introduction

The installation of the British in India in the mid-nineteenth century was not a unique phenomenon, for even a cursory glance at its past would show that, since time immemorial, the subcontinent has been regularly subjected to external invasions. There is that long historical cycle of the so-called Hindu period, spanning from 1,500 BC to 1,000 AD, that is beset with successive invasions by the Aryans, the Achaemenians, the Greeks, the Parthians, and the Huns.

There is then the relatively short cycle of the Muslim period, stretching from the Turkish raids in 1,000 AD until the steadfast installation of the British in the mid-nineteenth century— a period that includes invasions by the Turks, the Afghans and the Mughals trodding on the heels of each other.

Each of these invasions—many of which were "no more than smash-and grab raids"[1] have distinct characteristics of their own, and any discerning observer, listening to the sounds of history, should be able to identify the circumstances and the motivations that distinguish one from the other. Though this has already been done to some extent,[2] further incursions into India's past should highlight even more the singularity of each of these major periods of Indian history.

But all these successive forays, however, also bring into view some aspects that are common to all of them, and project a certain overall pattern which appears to establish a linkage between one invasion and the other.

The cultural level of the pre-British invaders was no higher than those who were invaded; if anything, it was lower; for there were areas of the subcontinent which, through the centuries, had developed civilisations of their own—civilisations that were clearly superior to those of the invaders. Consider the village sites of the Baluchistan hills before 2,500 BC, and consider the developed village communities along the rivers in Rajasthan and the Punjab. But, even more important than all this, think of the spectacular Indus valley or the Harappa civilisations in 2,500 BC which covered a much greater area than any other civilisation of antiquity known to mankind, and which had a remarkably developed system of towns and cities with proper roads, advanced drainage systems, robust brick houses and extensive storage facilities for grain. With the exception of the Greeks, known for their lush and rich history and some Mughal emperors, noted for their noteworthiness in architecture, the strength of the invaders, thus, lay not so much in the cultural-civilisational advancements as in their armed forces. For it was indeed not uncommon that the invasive history of the centuries that have gone by, the aggressive power of the sword did not necessarily mirror the civilisational level of a society. The gap was often too wide between the civil society and the military clout the country had acquired. To effectuate a focus on arms in a society can result from a whole series of factors, including the simple imperativeness to expand, to assert, to search for richer economies than their own, or the compelling drive of expansive religiosity, For how else can one explain the crusaders drive to conquer the holy land or the imperative Muslim motivation to convert the so-called "infidels."

The British Invasion

The British invasion was different. It was an experience that India had not encountered ever before. In effect, the invasion had created completely a new situation.

India had become a colony in the modern sense of the term. For the first time, a foreign power had neither come to plunder the riches of the nation and to return home, nor to find a new home to settle down, assimilating and fusing with the natives of the subcontinent. It had come as a growing industrial power to expand commerce, and slowly found itself, through the years—by the inherent logic of its expansive economic system—deeply involved in the process of physically conquering the entire land, and then ruling it in the interest of London.

The British occupation of the subcontinent also exposed the people to a different and technologically to a more developed civilisation. The impact was striking and brutal. While, on the one hand, it had contributed to the destruction "of the entire framework of Indian society" by breaking up the native communities, by uprooting the local industries, and by levelling all that was great and elevated in the native society thus separating India "from all its ancient traditions and from the whole of its past history;"[3] on the other hand, it had slowly unfolded a new process of advanced modernisation where legal uniformity was eventually instituted for the entire population, where the administration was centrally directed, where the government had become larger—perhaps more abstract and more secular—where loyalty to the nation slowly replaced the bonds of tribal, feudal or regional allegiances, and where self-contained units gave way to a larger and more impersonal organisation.

The very basis of economic life was also profoundly modified: mechanisation, emergence of industries, the opening of new markets, etc., signified the end of self-sufficient units based on home industries, craftsmanship and local market. New crops in agriculture, new technology in industries were introduced, and new pattern of relationships and transportation—with new inter-dependency—were established with the various regions of the world.

The traditional Indian structures, based on hierarchy, caste, privilege, were, to some extent, gradually swept away, and replaced by a new system of classes which were held together by a community of interests. New ideas, new opportunities, new ways of doing things, new lifestyles, and new aspirations that stemmed from extensive contacts with the west radically modified everyday life. Education and communications broke the small circle in which the individual once lived. His horizon was suddenly widened, and his circle of identification extended from the family to the tribe, to province and to the nation. These were thus the new underpinnings that India was exposed to.

The setting in of this acculturation process did not of course mean that India overnight had become a viable and a modern state. Far from it. It only meant that the British "as unconscious tools of history"[4] had spawned an irreversible process of a new pattern of modernisation that is continuing to this day.

All these developments were undoubtedly very significant. But, what was perhaps the most striking consequence of the establishment of a single political authority, of a uniform western-oriented educational system, and a developed communication network was that it brought the Indian elite in close contact with each other, and helped in the spawning of a new phenomenon—the phenomenon of a nationalist movement in the country. It had its small beginnings in the initial stages, but with the passage of time, and with the acceleration of the pace of modernisation, it acquired such dimensional strength, such an organisational capacity, and such massive support that it was no longer possible for the British to effectively rule single-handedly. Some understanding with the new emerging forces had become unavoidable. Only those empires sustain lengthily which are tolerant, and which are able to obtain the cooperation of the colonial people. This was indeed the case with the British Empire on the subcontinent.

Within the overall framework of the colonial rule, a number of attempts were, therefore, made in the twenties and thirties of the twentieth century to hold limited franchise elections, and to permit those elected to govern at the provincial levels, thus incorporating a segment of the Indian elite into the decision making process and assuring them that self-rule will be granted to the Indians. But, this was no longer acceptable to the Indians. They wanted more. They wanted complete independence, and that even as soon as possible.

Finally this is what happened. Due to a number of factors—including the considerable decline of Great Britain after World War II, power was finally handed over in 1947 after the subcontinent had been partitioned into the independent states of India and Pakistan.

Post-independence

The post-independent Indian history began with a concerted attempt to accelerate the pace of modernisation through programmatic planning, through an ever-widening role of the state in the economic and political development of the country, through modernised agriculture by land distribution, and through the transformation of socio-economic structures.

But, let it be noted that this gigantic effort to modernise, telescoping political and economic transformation, was carried out within a pluralistic political framework where the media is free, where political parties operate without any constraints, where fundamental human rights are guaranteed by an independent judiciary, where the checks and balances within the political system are effectively maintained, and where the future of the country is decided by the people through a system of periodic free elections.

This is indeed a difficult and uncommon experience, for it should not be forgotten that the Western world took several centuries to go through the whole process; and the system of representative governments that finally came into effect were operationalised only after the a tumultuous industrial revolution. The beginnings of political democratic change in the traditional Western societies thus occurred only in the aftermath of the industrial revolution and not before. Consider the egregious plight of most of its subjects who had no political voice while the industrial revolution was forging ahead.

In India, it was the other way round. Political democracy was partially established before the Indian industrial revolution thus generating a swath of problems which no one in the past had experienced—problems of sluggishness, of political opposition, of ideological dissension, of massive strikes, etc., all of which rendered the whole process of development difficult to manage. Whatever criticism one may be tempted to level at the flaws of the Indian system, the Indian leadership, on the whole, has acted on the firm belief that gradual development, without violence, represented the most effective and lasting method of developing the Indian society. This predilection for peaceful gradualism, it is often stressed, is not only in line with India's own tradition of trying to absorb and reconcile various faiths, but is perhaps a real and unique attempt of a developing country to seek a developmental and organisational model that successfully absorbs and synthesises what is positive and great in other systems.

In this tentative study we, therefore, propose, first of all, to examine fleetingly, a swath of basic issues. For example, what was the dimension of the British impact on the Indian society? Can it really be considered as a major and lasting watershed in Indian history whose ramifications are visible in India of today? What was the nature of Indian nationalism, how did it evolve, and why did it take the direction it took? And what was the process and circumstances that led to Indian independence in 1947?

While dealing with the present, we propose to address to some basic problems that India is faced with since independence, including the pattern of their evolution, the dimensionality of the issues, and the probity of the leadership which has the responsibility of managing them. Has India, for example, really succeeded in its effort to establish a functioning and a viable democracy? Has the economy taken the great leap forward to meet the basic needs of the people? Has the Indian society moved away from its tradition-bound hierarchical structures, its casteism, its social inequalities, etc,.? What about the leadership—political, bureaucratic, economic and intellectual? What framework has it established, what direction has it given, and what probity has it shown in managing the affairs of India? And, finally what about the new group of classes which are collaterally emerging as India goes forward industrially, and as it attempts move apace in the 21st century.

Obviously reflections on these dimensional issues can only be tentative, for some of them are too recent, and the documentation too fragmentary, to permit a definite evaluation of its past and its future.

Nevertheless, we cannot just wait for the dust to settle, for the time to pass, for archives to surface before analysing the period of its recent history, for the experiment currently being carried out by contemporary India is far too unique, far too important and far too relevant to the present epoch to be simply left to the deposits of history.

All history, in the eyes of B. Croce, is "contemporary history," that sees essentially "the past ...howsoever remote...through the eyes of the present and in the light of its problems."[5] The British historian, Collingwood, is perhaps even more relevant to our approach to recent history since we are neither concerned with "the past by itself" nor with the "historian's thought about it by itself" but with the "two things in their mutual relations".[6]

References

1. Lawrence James, *Raj : The Making of British India*, London: Abacus, 1997, p. 10.
2. John Keay, *The Honourable Company: A History of The English East India Company,* Harper Collins Publisher, 1995.
3. K. Marx and F. Engels, *On Colonialism,* Moscow: Foreign Languages Publishing House, 1960, p. 33.
4. Ibid., p. 37
5. Cited in E.H. Carr, *What is History,* London: Penguin Books, 1961, pp. 20-21.
6. Ibid., p. 21.

PART - I
THE PAST

1

Colonialism

You are not going to leave, I hope, the destinies of the British Empire to Prigs and Pedants

Benjamin Disraeli 1863

The British Empire in India was one of the great oddities of modern history. It was neither planned nor premeditated. It just happened. It was one of those slow and complex historical processes. It opened with the innocent founding of the British East India Company in 1600 for trade with the East, which developed into a powerful commercial institution with a massive network of trade interests in India and elsewhere, but which finally culminated in 1857 with the firm establishment of a vast empire embracing the whole of the subcontinent directly under the control of the British Government.

What was it that brought this transformation? How come that this commercial institution called the East India Company, founded for the purpose of establishing trade relations, slowly acquired the vocation of conquest? Was it really not possible for it to commercially flourish without indulging in political and military warfare? And how come that the Government in London decided to finally take over this mass of land, the size of Europe, with a population that was at least 30 times more than the Isles of England? Furthermore, what was the nature of British impact on traditional India? Did it bring to the Indian shores "the only social revolution ever heard of in Asia,"[1] as Marx has suggested, or did it actually retard a normal, independent growth of indigenous capitalism for which a basis apparently existed in the Indian socio-economic structure.

All these are undoubtedly important questions to which only tentative answers can be given through a faithful and relatively straight-forward description of the main events that took place during this period, and through a close analysis of the different forces that were struggling for influence in the area.

The East India Company

Originally the British East India Company was established to build up a trade of spices for which there had developed a fairly large market in England in the fifteenth and sixteenth centuries. The interests of the Company were first of all centred on the Indonesian islands, the foremost producers of spices at the time. But it did not take long, after its arrival in the area, before it received a bleak reception from its great competitors, the Dutch, who were already installed there, and who were determined to safeguard their monopolistic hold over trade. For them there was absolutely no scope for co-existence in the domain—least of all with the British who were considered as their adversaries, and whose decision to launch into spice trade was viewed with great alarm.

Under the circumstances, it was thus inevitable that friction would surge between these two great adversial European nations. Attacks were made on each other; a systematic campaign was launched against the interests of the other. And the whole situation finally culminated in the famous massacre of Amboyna in 1623 when the Dutch seized a British factory and mercilessly executed all its occupants. Thus ended the brief British episode to establish a major commercial presence in Indonesia, and it had to thereafter content itself with a marginal role in the area.

It was this Dutch success in preserving their Indonesian market that emboldened the British to search for other areas where they could commercially install themselves. The area they found for this purpose was the Indian subcontinent.

India, however, was considered the second best choice where disadvantages appeared to be equally insurmountable.

First of all, there were hardly any spices in the country to speak of except in the extreme South. There were of course other products like textile, saltpetre and sugar that were easily available. But, most of these items were bulky and more expensive to transport to faraway Europe. Second, like the Dutch in Indonesia, the Portuguese were already installed on the subcontinent, and appeared equally determined to keep the British out of India.

However, notwithstanding these difficulties, the British handled themselves in a much more subtle and, at the same time, more effective manner than was the case in Indonesia. Obviously, they had learnt from the setbacks at the hands of the Dutch. First of all they concentrated on the important objective of weakening the Portuguese power, the most visible adversary in the area. In it they were helped by three factors: (a) the unpopularity of the Portuguese whose control of the Arabian Sea and the Muslim pilgrim traffic was resented by the Mughals; (b) the waning of the Portuguese power due to difficulties in Europe, and (c) the significant rise in British maritime clout.

The first turning point came in 1612 when the Company's ships defeated the Portuguese in the swampy estuary of Surat. The Mughals were then willing to talk and an agreement was concluded in 1618 whereby the East India Company obtained important privileges in return for protection of the commercial and pilgrim sea traffic from the Portuguese; and the third turning point began with the siege of Ormuz—a strategic point in the Persian Gulf—jointly with the Persians and its capture in 1622 from the Portuguese after a heroic resistance. From this point onwards, the Company steadily developed its activities.

After having firmly established itself in Calcutta in 1620, in Madras in 1641 and in Bombay in 1663 an extensive campaign was launched to develop trade relations. From the information that is available of the period, it would seem that the rise of trade was steady but not spectacular, and that the pattern of trade was not limited to the much-needed spices but also extended to other items.

Imported to the West were items like cotton piece-goods, cotton yarn and indigo from Gujarat; from the Malabar coast came pepper and such other spices that could be bought second-hand from Ceylon and the east Indies; from Madras and Southeast Asia coast it was piece-goods and sugar, and from Bengal was available silk and saltpetre. In return, India bought metals such as tin, lead and quicksilver, novelties especially the mechanical ones, tapestries and ivories.

One of the striking aspect of this trade was the fact that the quantum of purchases made by India never equalled the purchases made by the Company from the subcontinent. The balance in favour of India had to be consequently paid by silver bullion. But this continuous drain of the bullion from England—obviously not a very healthy economic process in the seventeenth century—was viewed with great alarm by those who were at the helm of affairs in England. The company—perhaps for the first time—was under serious attack, and was spurred to seek some solution to the problem. The solution that was finally sought for an alternative means of payment was through the development of triangular trade relations. The Company, for instance, would sell Indian textiles to Sumatra, buy spices there, and dispose of some of them in London to continental buyers. In this manner it got its bullion from other sources than the British exchange reserves.

Political Role of the Company

Then in the eighteenth century, the political situation on the subcontinent began to undergo a change—a change to which the Company could hardly remain indifferent. The great Mughal empire, which covered practically the whole of India—with the exception of the south—began to collapse, rapidly loosing authority in areas over which it had exercised effective control for a long period of time. Everywhere disorder and instability began to spread. In many parts commercial activity was decreasing, and in some areas even travel was no longer possible as they were now infested with thieves and robbers. The problem was further compounded by the fact that in the immediate aftermath of the decline of the central Mughal authority provincial viceroys and governors moved forward to build their own small empires, owing only formal allegiance to Delhi.

The servants of the Company were now faced with a real dilemma. What should they do? Should they let the different Indian protagonists fight it out, and adopt a policy of benign neglect to the rapidly changing political situation? How should they cope with the rising problem of disorder in a country considered important for the development of commercial relations? And what about the French who were also increasingly asserting their presence in the south? Should they—their principal adversaries in Europe—be allowed to improve their position? Would this not affect the British position in Europe?

In the face of this difficult situation, the servants of the Company took a major decision: they decided to establish some law and order and to protect their interests by force, thus moving away from what was originally their principal vocation: trade. But this, it should be noted, was taken against the wishes and orders of the Directors in London, who realised how disastrous it would be for the profits to have to pay for force and armies, and, above all, wars. However notwithstanding this reluctance on the part of the central office, the East India Company representatives went ahead with their decision thus unfolding the process of conquering the whole of India.

This pattern of decisional dissidence would hardly be possible in this age and time, given the leap that has been made in communicational and transportation technology, whereas in the epoch of the East India Company such a decisional initiative had become unavoidably common.

One of the first major problems the Company had to deal with was the rising French presence in South India. The French East India Company, organised by Louis fourteenth's great Finance Minister, Colbert, had made remarkable progress between 1720 and 1740 by increasing the Company's trade ten times in value until it was nearly half that of the old-established British Company. French political influence had also increased. Under the able leadership of Duplex, the Governor-General of the French Company, the French were able to exercise a viable influence on the politics of the south.

A nation like France, with whom a conflict of interest was already developing in many areas of the world, an additional presence on the subcontinent, may endanger, the servants of the British Company feared, not only their specific interests in the area, but may well undermine the overall balance of power situation in the world.

With such a perception of the situation, the conflict between the two nations was obviously unavoidable in

India. It was only a question of time and preparedness before the already explosive situation would escalate into an actual conflict.

Interestingly enough it was the Anglo-French conflicts in Europe that provided the necessary catalysis for the development of conflicts on the subcontinent. The Austrian war of succession (1740-48) and the Seven Years War (1756-63), in which France and England found themselves on the opposite sides, had the spillover effect on India. In fact, one could argue that it was these two wars of wholly European origin that provided the major turning point in the history of modern India.

While the Austrian war was raging in Europe, a contest between the two East India Companies (English and French) began to develop. The arrival of the French fleet on the shores of India (1746) led to the capture of the important city of Madras. In 1748, the British Fleet retaliated by attacking Pondicherry, the important French possession. However, before a serious confrontation could develop, differences were tentatively resolved by the Treaty of Aix-la-Chapelle (1748) under which the city of Madras was returned to the British in exchange for the faraway Cape Briton island in North America. In appearance, the status quo was restored but in fact the two nations were preparing for a confrontation that finally took place in the South where both of them were endeavouring to place their own candidates on the two thrones that had become vacant. Through a series of daring military moves, under the leadership of Robert Clive, a supercilious and "a sturdy violent figure"[2] who turned out to be a genius for irregular warfare, the French forces were defeated at Trichinopoly. The final phase of the Anglo-French rivalry in India—collateral to the Seven Years War—opened with the attempt on the part of the French forces to occupy the city of Madras in 1758. However, the French, crippled as they were with jealousies and bad leadership, failed in this major endeavour, and were finally and decisively defeated at Wandiwash in 1760 where du Bussy, the French Commander, was taken prisoner.

Empire Building

This was the real end of the French bid for control of the Indian subcontinent; the road was now wide open for the British to launch their great adventure of slowly and steadily occupying India without any interference from their European enemies.

The first area to be brought under control was the eastern region of which Bengal was the most important centre. The Hindu merchants in Calcutta had apparently joined the local British population in a conspiracy against the local Viceroy of the area. Whether this was in fact the case of course still remains an open question. In any event what is clear is that the Viceroy was convinced about the conspiracy between the Hindu merchants and the British, and decided to take revenge by attacking the city of Calcutta which had by then become a major centre of British settlement in India. In the fighting that ensued the city was captured and the English who had remained behind were imprisoned.

There then took place that senseless tragedy called the "the black hole of Calcutta" under which 146 Englishmen were confined to a cell in a fort which was no more than 18 feet long and 14 feet wide, and which had only one small and narrow window. Only 23 came out alive next morning, the rest having suffocated to death.

When this tragic news arrived in Madras, the centre of British military presence, an expedition was rapidly despatched to Calcutta under the leadership of Clive and Watson. The city of Calcutta was rapidly recovered, and one daring attack on the incredibly large forces of Viceroy created complete confusion in the ranks of the Indian troops, and led them to withdraw to the north. Events now moved with telescopic speed, reaching a climax at the famous battle of Plassey (1757) where, betrayed by his own general, the Viceroy suffered one humiliating defeat after the other. The war was over and with it the door was then opened for the establishment of the British Empire.

Plassey, "the most miserable skirmish ever to be called a decisive battle."[3] nonetheless was a political landmark in so far as the East India Company became the owner of nearly nine hundred square miles of territory to the south of Calcutta, thus acquiring the de facto status of a king- maker in Bengal.

A puppet Viceroy, Nazim, was installed from 1757 to 1772. It was during these fifteen years that the whole area was subjected to organised loot and plunder by the mercantile company, and its servants, actively assisted and encouraged by the Hindu commercial class who shared the loot with them. There is no instance known—at least in Indian history—where a great province was swept so clean of its wealth. "The trade of the country merchant," confirms an Indian historian, N.K. Sinha, "began to stagnate. Armenian, Mughul, Gujarati and Bengali merchants found their free trade daily fettered and loaded. The export import, manufacturing of goods had moved from the hands of independent merchants to intermediaries hired by the East India Company. Equally worse was the decision to impose the Company's monopoly on the country's inland trade."[4]

This open interference in the affairs of Bengal also brought the imperial Mughul forces in the field. The encounter between the Company's forces and the imperial army at Buxar (1765) ended in the defeat of the Mughuls. The Mughul emperor, installed in Delhi, now formally recognised the changes brought about by the battle of Plassey, and entrusted Robert Clive, who was then the Governor of Bengal, the responsibility of revenue administration of Bengal, Bihar and Orissa.

Thus the East India Company became sovereign of three provinces two of which were among the richest in India. It controlled the mouth of the Ganges, and thereby the entire maritime trade of the Gangetic valley which flowed into the new port of Calcutta. The Company was now in a position to make a bid for the rest of India. For the next two decades it followed a policy of taking over the neighbouring princely States with the first subsidiary treaty that was negotiated with the great province of Oudh. Gradually, the Maratha empire, which alone posed a serious threat to the growing pretensions of the British company, was isolated, and in 1803 Arthur Wellesley, later Duke of Wellington, defeated the combined forces of the Maratha States at the battle of Assaye. Though the only power capable of challenging its empire was thus laid low, its threat was not completely eliminated till 1818, when in a final war, the Maratha power was swept away from its home domains annexed to the possessions of the Company in Bombay.

Henceforth the British became the unchallenged sovereign of a great part of India, governing the country directly or through puppet or subsidiary princes. The Punjab and some outlying provinces were still beyond their control, but the empire had become an established fact and the subsequent wars with the Sikhs and Gurkhas and the Burmese in Burma rounded it off on the map.

From the hindsight we have now acquired, and the documentation that is available of this great episode of empire-building, one could venture to suggest that many of these conquests were the result of initiatives taken by the men-on-the-spot—often without consultation, and, more often than not, in defiance of the wishes of those ruling England and the Company. It was the reflection of the age when transportation was slow moving, when communication was dilatory, and when information in the hands of the faraway rulers was nugatory. It was man-on-the-spot who was the great decisional actor.

The reasons that led the servants of the East India Company in India to expand the empire were of course varied. There was Warren Hastings (1774-1785) who was simply looking for peace on his restless borders; there was Arthur Wellesley (1798-1804) who had a fixation about the French in India; and there was James Andrew Dalhousie (1848-1856) who could not stand badly administered States.

In other words, it was the man-on-the-spot who made the empire and not the British Government. It was he who plundered the riches of the country; it was he who conjured up visions of building an empire, of systematically destroying local kingdoms, of initiating military campaigns that were pregnant with political consequences, and of taking major political decisions.

In fact, it was thanks to the incorrigible pioneering work of the company's servant that the British Empire acquired its peculiarly diffuse character; for "but for the company there would have been not only no British India, but also no British Empire."[5]

However, if the servants of the East India Company were the real empire-builders, it was the British Government in London that slowly assumed the responsibility of running the country; for this business of administering this huge country was too serious a matter to be left in the hands of the local empire-builders who had no experience in real governance. The process of taking over had already begun in 1784 with the establishment of a Board of Control and with the appointment of the governor-general by London. The Government of India acts of 1813, 1833 and 1853 through which the governor-general exercised a control over the Company further accelerated it. After the Indian revolt of 1857, the British Government went even further—in fact much further. It abolished the Company,[6] and itself took over the great task and responsibility of administering this great landmass, the size of Europe, with a population of more than three hundred million people. This was the greatest act of empire building.

Ramifications of Colonialism

What was the effect of all this on India? How did the Indian customs, mode of life, culture, etc., face up to this new dynamic and technologically oriented civilisation. Was the whole society severely shaken, or was it able to effectively confront and adapt itself to the exigencies of the new system?

The Dark Side

The cosmic character of Western civilisation, under which several societal aspects of its subjects was scrutinised, influenced and severely shaken, could hardly leave the traditional, and hitherto closed Indian structures unaffected. In fact, they were shaken—severely shaken.

The sources of national wealth were, first of all, severely narrowed down under British impact. In the nineteenth century, pre-British India was a highly developed manufacturing country exporting its manufactured products to Europe and other continents. Its banking system was efficient and well organised throughout the country, and the bills of exchange, issued by the great businesses or financial houses were valid everywhere in the country, as well as in Iran, Afghanistan, and Central Asia. Merchant capital had emerged, and there was already an elaborate network of agents, jobbers, brokers and middlemen. The ship building industry was flourishing, and one of the English flagships was built by an Indian firm during the Napoleonic wars. In fact, India was as advanced industrially, commercially and financially, as any country prior to the industrial revolution.

Observers have written that many accounts or travels vouch for this state of affairs. J. Pirenne confirmed this in his writing of the nineteen fifties. He wrote:

> In the middle of the seventeenth century, Asia still had a far more important place in the world than Europe. The riches of Asia were incomparably greater than those of the European States. Her industrial technique showed a subtlety and a tradition that the European handicrafts did not possess. And there was nothing in the more modern method used by the traders of the Western countries that the Asian traders had to envy. In matters of credit, transfer of funds, insurance and cartels neither India, non Persia nor China had anything to learn from Europe.[7]

Adam Smith, towards the third quarter of the eighteenth century, spoke of the "wonderful accounts of the wealth and cultivation" of India and underlined the fame it had acquired for its "superiority in agriculture and manufactures"[8] The French traveller, Jean- Baptiste Tavernier, who visited India in the middle of the seventeenth century writes about Kassimbazar, a village in Bengal which could "furnish about twenty two thousand bales of silk annually, each bale weighing one hundred livres."[9] He was also impressed by the fact that "business is conducted with freedom and fidelity."[10] Describing a diamond mine in Kolkar near Golekunda (South India) Tavernier writes: "there were close upon 60,000 persons who worked there, including men, women and children, who were employed in diverse ways, the men in digging, the women and children in carrying earth."[11] A little later (1656-83) when another Frenchman, F. Bernier, visited India, he was struck by the fact that there was no other country where so much variety could be found. Referring to the abundance of cotton and silk in Bengal he wrote: "the Kingdom called the common storehouse of these two kinds of merchandise not only for the empire of the great Mogul, but of all the neighbouring kingdoms and even of Europe".[12] Discussing a workshop, he observed, "The Dutch have sometimes seven or eight hundred natives employed in their silk factory at Kassimbazar, where in like manner the English and other merchants employ a proportionate number."[13]

The East India Company destroyed all this. Its commercial policy of more than hundred years systematically discouraged Indian manufactured goods. Its fixed policy, pursued during the last decades of the eighteenth and the first decades of the nineteenth centuries, was to make India subservient to the industries of Great Britain pushing the colony to grow raw materials only to supply material for the British looms and manufacturers. This policy was pursued with unwavering resolution and with fatal success; orders were sent out to force Indian artisans to work in the Company's factories, commercial residents were vested with extensive power over villages and communities of Indian weavers, prohibitive tariffs excluded Indian silk and cotton goods from England, and English goods were admitted into India free of duty or on payment of a nominal duty.

The British manufacturers, in the words of the historian, H.H. Wilson, "employed the arm of political justice to keep down and ultimately strangle a competitor with whom he could not have contented with equal terms."[14]

Millions of Indian artisans lost their earnings and India lost one of the great sources of wealth. The invention of the power-loom in Europe completed the decline of Indian industries; and when the power-loom was subsequently set up in India, England once more acted towards India with unfair jealousy. An excise duty was then imposed on the production of cotton fabrics in India thus disabling the Indian manufacturers from competing with the manufacturers of Japan and China and stifling the new steam mills of India.

Agriculture was then virtually the only remaining source of national wealth, and approximately four-fifths of the people depended on it. Here too a land tax was levied which was not only excessive but also fluctuating and uncertain. In England the land tax was between one and four shillings to the pound; that is to say 5 to 20 percent of the rental during a hundred years between 1798 and 1898 when it was made perpetual and redeemable. In Bengal the land tax was fixed at over 90 per cent on the rental, and in northern India at over 80 per cent of the rental between 1798 and 1882, Admittedly, the British Government only followed the precedent of the previous Muslim rulers who were also notorious for claiming an enormous land tax. But there was a difference in the effectiveness of such an action: whereas what the Muslim rulers claimed they could never fully realise, the British realised fully and with rigour. They had the power.

The last Muslim ruler of Bengal, during the last years of his administration (1764), realised a land revenue of 817,553 pounds within thirty years, whereas the British realised a land revenue of 2, 680,000pounds in the same province. In Madras, the land tax first imposed by the East India Company was one-half of the gross produce of the land. In Bombay, the land revenue of the territory conquered from the Maharattas in 1817 was 800,000 pounds in the year of the conquest. This was raised to 1, 500,000 pounds within a few years, and it was continuously raised since then. "No native prince demands the rent which we do," wrote Bishop Herber in 1926 after travelling through India.[15] "A land tax that which now exists in India" wrote Colonel Briggs in 1830, "professing to absorb the whole of the Landlord's rent was never known under any government in Europe or Asia."[16]

From all this it would appear that the East India Company considered the subcontinent as a vast personal estate or plantation, the profits of which were withdrawn from India and deposited in Europe. It reserved all the high appointments in India for its nominees seeking a lucrative career in the east. It bought its merchandise out of the revenues of India and sold it to Europe for its own profit. It vigorously exacted from India a high interest on its stock-in-trade. In one shape or another all that could be raised in India by an excessive taxation flowed to Europe after paying for a starved administration.

Finally, the East India Company's vocation of trade was abolished in 1833 and it ceased to exist in 1859. But, its capital was paid off by loans that were made into an Indian debt on which interest was paid from Indian taxes. The empire was transferred from the Company to the Crown, but it was the people of India who paid the purchase money. The Indian debt, which was 51,000,000 pounds in 1857 rose to 97,000,000 pounds in 1862. But this was not all; it continued to rise, reaching the astronomical figure of 200,000,000 pounds by 1901.

What was the effect of this economic drain from India to England. Did it really fill the pockets of a few individuals or did it have a visible effect on British economy and British development?

Without the Indian wealth, it has been argued, it would not have been possible for the industrial revolution to really take off in Britain. Inventions alone—though obviously important—were by no means enough to transform the economy of any nation unless and until it has been closely integrated with the production system. For example "in 1733 Kay patented his fly-shuttle and in 1788 Wyatt patented his roller-spinning machine worked by water power; but neither of these inventions seem to have come to use"[17] But later all this changed. The appearance of Hargreave's spinning jenny in 1770, Arkwright's water-powered spinning frame in 1769, and the application of the steam engine to blast furnace in 1785 heralded the dawn of the industrial revolution. Why? Because after Plassey (1757) Indian wealth began to be systematically channelled to England. Adam Brook's testimony amply proves this point. "Before the influx of Indian treasure, and the expansion of credit that followed, no force sufficient for this purpose existed, and had Wyatt lived fifty years earlier, he and his inventions must have perished together. Possibly since the world began, no investment has ever yielded the profit reaped from the Indian plunder, because for nearly fifty years Great Britain stood without a competitor. From 1694 to Plassey (1757) the growth had been relatively slow. Between 1760 and 1815 the growth was very rapid and prodigious."[18]

At this point one may validly ask: what if India had managed to escape British rule? What if it had been able to develop and evolve on its own steam with its own genius and without any interference from the outside? Would it have remained an idyllic and pre-industrial nation without any prospects of developing viably? Would capitalism not have emerged from India's own socio-political structures?

An elementary knowledge of economic history is enough to demonstrate that capitalism does not just come. It grows; and unless British rule can be equated with the totality of creative forces of world history, capitalism in India could have grown even if there had been no Plassey and no Clive. Indian society was already in the process of disintegrating because of the endogenous factors, and British rule as a exogenous factor only accelerated this process, just as the Roman invasion had accelerated the fall of the slave society in the west. Indeed it has been argued that the British invasion had in fact thwarted the normal course of Indian evolution. Bourgeois rule, that was growing within the shell of the old order; "But foreign bourgeois rule," writes R.P. Dutt, "forcibly superimposing itself on the old society, and smashing the germs of the rising

India bourgeois class- Herein lay the tragedy of Indian development which thereafter became a thwarted or distorted social development for the benefit of a foreign bourgeoisie."[19]

But this was not all that impoverished India under the British. There was also the establishment of the Indian armed forces which were "kept at a strength much beyond what the defence of the country" required[20]—a strength that was principally used for British imperial expansion beyond the borders of India.

The greatest cause, however, was the steady drain of wealth from India to England—a drain that included pensions sent to England, interests drawn in England on investments made in India, business profits made in India. etc. "A sum," wrote R.C. Dutt, "reckoned at twenty millions of English money, or a hundred million of American money, (some other authorities put it much higher), which, it should be borne in mind is equal to half the net revenues, is remitted annually from this country (India) to England without a direct equivalent. Think of it! One- half of what we (in India) pay as taxes goes out of the country, and does not come back to the people. No other country on earth suffers like that at the present day; and no other country on earth could bear such an annual drain without increasing impoverishment and repeated famines. We denounce ancient Rome for impoverishing Gaul and Egypt, Sicily and Palestine, to enrich herself. We denounce Spain for robbing the new world and the Netherlands to amass wealth. England is following exactly the same practice in India. Is it strange that she is converting India into a land of poverty and famine."[21]

Poverty and famine thus was what India had to reckon with—so much so that it had to face a succession of famines. "During the eighty years of the nineteenth century," confirmed W.C. Lilly, who had long served in India, "18,000, 000 people perished of famine. In one year alone, when her late Majesty assumed the title of Empress, 5,000,000 people in Southern India were starved to death. In the district of Bellary, with which I am personally acquainted –a region twice the size of Wales—one fourth of the population perished in the famine of 1816-77. I shall never forget my own famine experience: how as I rode out on horseback, morning after morning, I passed crowds of wandering skeletons, and saw human corpses by the roadside, unburied, uncared for, and half devoured by dogs and vultures; how sadder sight still, children 'the joy of the world' as the old Greeks deemed, had become its ineffable sorrow and were forsaken by the very women who had borne them, wolfish hunger killing even the maternal instinct...."[22]

The Bright Side

But can one really argue—as many do—that this British invasion and occupation of the subcontinent brought nothing but misery to the people of India, that it economically drained the land, that it "broke down the entire framework of Indian society without any symptom of reconstitution yet appearing,"[23] that it undermined the balance that existed between agriculture and industry, and that it eliminated all hope of a real indigenous industrial revolution.

Undoubtedly, much of this is true: for even a superficial glance at the British record in India amply shows the unparalleled and brutal destruction of Indian structures.

But, this is not the whole story. There is the other side of the coin that appears to be less destructive and less negative. In fact, there are some like Marx who—while underlining the destructive aspects of British imperialism—considered that the demolition of traditional structures by the British was "the only social revolution ever heard of in Asia, and that the laying of the material foundations of Western society on the subcontinent was accomplished by the British as "the unconscious tools of history."[24]

Whether they were "unconscious tools of history" or not, the first dramatic and palpable ramification of British invasion was that it ended the 700 year old Muslim rule in India. By itself this was a major landmark event—undoubtedly a milestone in Indian history. The Hindu majority had shown a total incapacity of defying the Muslim establishment or grabbing power from the Muslim rulers. There were some isolated attempts to do so, but none of them were successful. Shivaji was perhaps the most exalted example of this defiance, but this did not result in conspicuous victory.

The passive Hindus needed a deliverer; and paradoxically it was the British colonial invaders who performed this role. They came as invaders, but finally ended as deliverers.

To risk a generalisation, it could be argued that the 700 years of Muslim rule did not have any great positive impact in terms of establishing an efficacious and sound government, or in terms of establishing friendly bridges with the local population. If anything, Muslim rule was notorious for its Islamic identity, and for the imposition of juridico-administrative system that systematically challenged and pitilessly destroyed the existing system of social conduct, culture, religious practices, lifestyles and ethically codes of conduct, not to speak of the forcible conversions that some of the Hindus had to endure. The Islamic fundamentalism, which the Muslim establishment believed in, and to which it adhered to, resulted in the generation of second class status for the Hindu majority.

All this should be kept in mind while evaluating the British colonial rule. In his influential novel *Anandamath* (1882) Bankim Chandra Chatterjee, the Hindu leaders appeared to be struggling not against the British who had supposedly come as liberators, but against Muslim tyranny and misrule.

1 *Political Unity*

In the first place the political unity of India was more consolidated and extended even further than it ever was under the great Mughuls. For the first time in its entire history the whole of the subcontinent—reaching the natural land and sea frontiers—was brought under the control of one administration. Even the princely Indian States, still ruled by the Maharajas with far-reaching autonomy in their internal administration of things, became, for all practical purposes, a part of India. They had really no power and no authority except what was attributed to them by the British.

This unity, imposed by the British sword, was subsequently strengthened by a remarkable development in the means of transportation and communication. The first telegraph line was opened in 1852, and by 1938-39 there were 93,190 miles of telegraph lines and 470, 108 miles of telegraph wires. Telephone exchanges in the big cities of Bombay, Calcutta, Madras and Karachi were already opened in 1881-1882; and slowly with the movement of time they covered all the principal centres of the subcontinent. But it was the construction of an extensive system of roads and railways that really gave a new dimension to the new unity of India. The first railway line between Bombay and Thana was opened to the traffic in 1853, and by 1859 it covered 5,015 miles by railway tracks. In 1939 41,134 miles of railways were at work. Roads too developed significantly. It was estimated that there were about 20,000 miles of surfaced road in the country in 1880, and they reached the impressive figure of 50,000 miles at the beginning of World War I. Thus, for the first time in the history of India the revolution in the means of transport and communications opened areas beyond one's immediate environment thus spawning the possibilities for the psychological unification of the vast subcontinent.

Whatever motivations one may attribute to the British decision to initiate such a technological revolution in the country, it is undeniable that it greatly contributed to the slow emergence of a sense of an identity that is invariably a significant precursor to the feeling of becoming a great nation. People began to travel, goods began to move faster, and ideas began to journey across the land.

Security

The British Raj also made it possible for the nation to acquire a feeling of security—a security India never had, since it had been a constant target of invasions and plunder. It is indeed remarkable that once the subcontinent became a part of the empire one of the major preoccupations of the British was to defend it against any outside attack. In fact, the defence of India dominated British policy, and significantly influenced British diplomacy. This involved Britain in a series of little wars: it took a war to conquer Sind, two to takeover the Punjab, three to subjugate Burma, another three to keep Afghanistan a friendly buffer State. Occasionally, there were conflicts that did not remain restricted, for there were situations that involved other international actors. In 1895-96 there was trouble with France on the Upper Mekong. In 1855 the pacific Gladstone called out reserves during the quarrel with Russia over the demarcation of Afghanistan's northern borders.

That the British discharged this burdensome responsibility successfully is evident from the fact that the nation, blessed with natural boundaries of the mountains and the seas, was finally ringed by dependent protectorates and buffer States like Persia, Afghanistan, Tibet, Nepal, Sikkim, Bhutan and Burma. The only real threat emanated from Russia. Here again British policy was deeply influenced by this threat. It fought the Second Afghan war, created the Penjedeh incident, and was constantly involved in the little frontier wars of the 90s.

Some writers of this period of British-Indian history have in fact even gone further, and have suggested that British policies in Africa, in the Persian Gulf, in Southeast Asia, and, to some extent, even in

Europe, were influenced and affected by British interests in India.[25]

Admittedly, all these efforts to defend India were primarily taken with the specific purpose of safeguarding British imperial interests rather than those of the Indians. Admittedly, all these actions were clearly imperialistic policies of which the Indian army was the principal oppressive instrument. Nonetheless, it would be difficult to deny that India did not reap some advantage out of these policies; for it did have peace and security during the entire period of British rule. There were indeed no invasions.

New Administration

In internal affairs too, British impact was significant. During the time of the East India Company vast administrative machinery was established, the foundations of which were laid by Cornwallis.

The period that followed the 1857 revolt witnessed the growth and development of administrative machinery that has no parallel in the history of the world. Neither the Byzantine nor the Chinese empires, both typically bureaucratic, produced anything that was comparable to the great administrative service built up in the country. The British also governed the land by assuming the function of the politicians, and by undertaking "the greater and more positive function of carrying the people"[26] with them. With the administrative machinery so organised the government was able to take up the work of the administration on a scale no government outside Russia had undertaken. Railways, roads and telegraph lines knit the country together. Great irrigation schemes were undertaken notably in the Punjab and the United Provinces (UP). Peace reigned over the land and law was administered under a system of jurisprudence that was enlightened and comprehensive. The land revenue system was overhauled, and though an uneconomic system of landlordism prevailed in many parts, the settlements and assessment of lands and the demands of the government were clearly defined. In fact, for a hundred years India had a peaceful administration.

The unavoidable ramification of such a gigantic growth was "the hypertrophy of the bureaucratic methods of administration."[27] The bureaucratic machinery did become cumbersome, an elaborate system of red tape did slow the governing process, and *Babuism* did hamper the efficient functioning of the bureaucracy "on all sides by precedents, vested interests and ancient customs."[28] Many British administrators, including Lord Curzon, were scandalised by this growth, but this was the price that had to be paid, given the dimension of the country, and given the absence of any system of organised governance during the period to which the British could have latched onto.

Innovative Education

British policy in the educational sphere also produced certain far-reaching effects. In the beginning up to 1813, the East India Company had followed the traditional pattern of governmental patronage to Indian learning, though on a much more modest scale than the Mughals. There was Warren Hasting's college of Arabic and Persian studies in Calcutta, and there was Jonathan Duncan's Sanskrit college in Benares. But this concentration on Indian classics and Indian culture did not last long, for with the arrival of Lord William Bentinck, the new Governor General on the scene, a new policy was put forward. He had a different frame of mind, and a different concept of what India needed in terms of education. For him the English Language was "the key to all improvements," and general education was the real "panacea for the regeneration of India." He found support in the India House in London from James Mill who was convinced of the importance of Westernisation and who had developed a passion for "useful knowledge." Later the reforming Whig ministry, with its radical tendencies, also became a proponent of this new educational trend. In Calcutta in 1834 Bentinck received support from forward-looking Indian intellectuals, led by Ram Mohan Roy, who had helped to found a college for Western learning. The most powerful reinforcement, however, came with the arrival of Thomas Babington Macaulay in 1834 who, as the son of an eminent evangelical leader, fervently advocated the utilisation of funds, earmarked for education, for the pursuit of knowledge that was worth knowing; and he had no doubt whatever that English was more worth knowing than Sanskrit and Arabic. His object, as he put it, was to "create a class of persons Indians in colour and blood, but English in tastes, in opinion, in morals and in intellect,[29] arguing that "a single shelf of good European Library was worth the whole native literature of India and Arabia."[30]

The result of all this was the decision to launch English education and Western knowledge into India- a decision unique in colonial annals of Asia of that time. Just before his retirement in 1835 Bentinck declared that "the great object of the British Government ought to be the promotion of European literature and science among the people of India, and that funds appropriated to education would be best employed in English education"[31] From this point on the government began to set up schools and colleges imparting Western Education in the English language. To this was added another measure of greatest importance. English replaced Persian (the court language of the Mughuls) as the official state language and the medium of the higher courts of law with the local language replacing Persian in lower courts. By one stroke the learning of English was given a great stimulus; its cultivation clearly involved contact with Western ideas and values of which it was the vehicle. At the same time the local languages were brought down from poetry to prose, and were given a function and a status which has led to their modern development.

Western science was specifically introduced in the form of Western medicine of which the Calcutta medical college (1836) and the engineering college in Rurkee (1849) were the first institutions. Science also received attention in both schools and colleges. Western technology spread through engineering works like roads, canals and later railways with the Indians trained to build and administer them. The process was accelerated by the increase in the number of Indians entering the administration. Thus this educational policy amounted in effect to a presentation of the West to the East. Of course, it was an English version of the west, and the presentation from one small elite to another.

It was of course easy to go out into the countryside, and say that traditional life went on just as before; it was evidently easy to laugh at some of the early cultural hybrids; it might even have seemed smart to declare that when the two cultures met, each borrowed the worst of the other. These things were said for many years, but the fact remains that these measures began a creative contact between the two countries, which was to transform India within a century. However, in addition to these meetings of the East and the West, it made another lasting contribution: it created a large body of like-minded elite all over multilingual India, who spoke the same language, had the same point of view and was able to psychologically think of the subcontinent in terms of one country.

Discovery of the Past

In other fields too the British achievements were also notable. They made the Indians conscious of the greatness of their past. In the eighteenth century, on the eve of the establishment of British rule, the Hindus had no recollection of their real past—none whatsoever— no established tradition for historical research, no interest in their past, and no idea of the true character of the classical Sanskritic civilisation. Their Hinduism was a broken-up and a simplified version of Hinduism of ancient India. It was unorganised in space and unsupported in time. Its quality was neutral where it was not purely negative.

It was the Europeans who began to discover India's past. In 1837 James Princep discovered the clue to the inscriptions of Ashoka. This was an event that revolutionised Indian history, for it provided the key to a systematic study of ancient India. In 1860 Alexander Cunnigham was appointed the first director of

Archaeology. This emboldened and catalysed the whole process of discovering the past, while Fergusson's monumental work describing the magnificent architectural monuments of India laid the foundation for the revival of Indian interests in arts.

The appointment of Dr. Hultz as epigraphist to the Government of India was the beginning of the great work of reclamation of Indian history. The deciphering of the ancient Indian scripts, and the official search for inscriptions all over the country, and their publication gave India the first corpus of material from which its history could be reconstructed. It is almost an epic story, and its significance in generating among Indians a historical sense of pride in their achievements cannot be overrated. Today when we talk of the Mauryas, the Guptas, the Chalukyas and the Pallavas, let it be remembered that the story of these great ages of Indian history was recovered by the devoted labours of European scholars in the service of the British Government in India.

If Indian history was recovered, so were the two other main streams of thought: Buddhism and Pali literature. For a thousand years Buddha had been forgotten. To the Hindus he was one of the minor avatars of Hinduism. It was the work of the European scholars that resuscitated him. The great king Ashoka, whose name seemed to have been expunged from Indian history, was restored to his honours, and today holds a position in the minds of Indians higher than any other monarch—the result not of Indian researches but that of European scholars. Even the revival of Sanskrit studies on modern lines is largely due to the activities of the British Government, and the scholars patronised by it. The Queen's college at Benares was the first serious attempt to teach Sanskrit in a systematic way to young Indians, and it is a fact worthy of note that even the great religious classics of India—the Vedas, the Upanishads, the Dharma Shastras have been made available to a much wider circle than ever before through the critical translation by European scholars.

This is also the case in regard to Indian art and sculpture. In the beginning of the 19th century, Ellora, Ajanta and Mahabalipuram meant nothing to Indians, nor did the magnificent sculptures of Elephanta and temples of Orissa. It is to men like Havell and Coomaraswamy (an anglo-tamil born and bred in Britain) that India owes the revival of Indian artistic sense. These are undoubtedly achievements to the credit of the British whose values will greatly increase as the time goes by.

The resuscitation of the past, in the words of an Indian writer has "fired the imagination of the Hindus, and made them conscious of a heritage of their own which they could pit not only against the Muslims but also against that of the far more powerful and virile English, Psychologically, the Indian people crossed the line which divides primitive peoples from civilised peoples, They could now be said to belong to the same species as the Homo Sapiens historicus of Europe."[32]

Rule of Law

Almost as significant as the introduction of English or political unity or the cultural discovery of India was the establishment of the rule of law. This ensured—at least theoretically— the equality of all men irrespective of their caste, and affirmed the individual right of the individual. Hitherto, Hinduism had differentiated between Brahmin and non-Brahmin, while Islam observed one law for the Muslims and another for the "infidels". The influence of this highly complex and fairly well organised institution on Indian life was more lasting than all the influences indicated above. The values implied in its rules and procedures have enjoyed much greater immunity from political attack. Though there were some opinions in the Indian nationalist movement that favoured the boycott of the courts, it was never strong enough to encourage this process, There have been Britishers who doubted the suitability of English ideas of impartiality and evidence for Indian conditions; and it may well be that the results of the process of law were different from those originally intended. Though the political effects of hundred years growth of the legal profession, and the emergence of separate judicial ethos in India have never been fully explored, one thing is certain: it did have an impact at the leadership level in so far as there was a real preponderance of lawyers among top Indian politicians. This drew scorn and distrust from the British administrators who often regarded lawyers as unrepresentative of the Indian people as a whole, and too prone to embrace criticism for its own sake. But, they overlooked the positive effect of this preponderance of law—a preponderance that resulted in the establishment of a fairly large political group which became accustomed to the world of rules and resistant to arbitrary autocracy. But, the impact was also visible at the lower levels of small town pleaders who performed the vital function of making a bridge between traditional and modern values. While they operated professionally in the modern setting of the courts, their clients were embedded in ancient custom. It was the small lawyer who kept rural India at least in faint touch with the cities where new political ideas were emerging. Hired to manipulate the mysteries of the foreign legal system, he was able to communicate the ethos of the system to his clients.

Here then was a fixed set of standards embodied in and upheld by established independent institutions: that the parties to the dispute stand equal in the eyes of law and have equal access to law; that the accused person is innocent until found guilty; that the evidence must be brought forward and sifted before an impartial judge; that the duty of the judge is to administer law having regard to the principles of natural justice, and with an indifference to the convenience of the politically and otherwise powerful. All these values, while not native to the Indian soil, nonetheless conquered the minds of the educated Indians, and the nationalist movement drew some of its leading members from the ranks of the legal profession (Gandhi, Nehru, Jinnah, Patel, etc.) It is therefore little wonder that the legacy was taken over with respectful care, as was evident in the debates of the Indian Constituent Assembly after the independence of the country in 1947, in the Constitution's provisions concerning the judiciary, and in the tone of most of the documents. Even the inclusion of fundamental rights was not so much an imitation of other constitutions as it was a tribute to the judiciary in India and the values it preached over a century.

Democracy and Self Governing Institutions

Another striking legacy of the British rule was the introduction of political freedom, and the slow but nonetheless steady emergence of institutions that finally led the nation to have an organised and stable transition to independence in 1947.

In the early days of the British rule, the European community in India enjoyed the rights of free association, of open criticism of the government, of the freedom of the press. But, gradually with the development of India these rights were extended to the elitist Indians. They too were permitted to organise themselves politically, to freely express their aspirations, to openly voice their demands, and to criticise the imperial Government uninhibitedly.

Admittedly, there were periods of repression, brutal massacres and massive arrests. Admittedly, there were times when the British clamped down on the critical press, banned the political parties, imprisoned its leaders, and declared the whole of Indian subcontinent as an emergency area totally deprived of any right of free expression. Even a cursory glance at the British rule would show signs of marked repression. But, who, on the other hand, can deny those long periods when political agitation was allowed, when the nationalist press was permitted to pour out its criticism against British rule, when political parties were treated with great courtesy, and when they were freely allowed to travel both inside and outside the country to propagate their nationalistic ideals?

All these rights, acquired by the Indians through the years, are often attributed to the political struggle that was carried out by them; this is undoubtedly true, for as we shall see in the following chapter, there was an indeed a long and continuous pressure exercised by the Indian nationalistic forces that contributed to the extension of liberal democracy in India. But, this is not the only reason, for there were other areas and other countries under the control of the colonial powers where such pressures did not lead to the introduction of liberal institutions. In this connection, consider the Spanish Empire builders in Latin America, the French in Africa and Indo-China, and the Dutch in Indonesia. In India, it was therefore not only the indigenous pressures that had something to do with the British and their own liberal institutions. Indeed the first three decades of the nineteenth century constitute an important period for British liberalism. It was the golden age of the reform bills, of catholic emancipation, of the abolition of slavery: it was the age of enlightened statesmen such as Burke, Pitt and Wilberforce in England, and Wellesley, Hastings, Munro, Malcolm, Elphinstone, Metcalfe and Bentinck in India, all filled with a deep sense of mission. To them goes the credit of raising the level of the administration of the East India Company to the pedestal of trusteeship. Even, while they were empire building, they were contemplating its end. The instability of empires—even the mightiest—was ever before their eyes, and their ideas about liberal government and its obligation towards the governed were cast in the loftiest model. None of them appears to have entertained the idea that Indians should not have institutions of their own which permits them to organise themselves, and which makes it possible for them to freely express their views.

Closely linked with the ideas of liberalism was another British legacy—the legacy of developing self-governing institutions which eventually made it possible for India to have an easy transition from colonial rule to that of political independence. For India, through this process, had acquired an experience of governance that was useful after independence.

The process had begun very modestly with the passing of the Indian Council's Act of 1861 under which Indians were appointed to the newly created Legislative Council. It gained some pace with the introduction of the local self-government institutions in 1883, and the acceptance in 1909 of the principle of elections for the Governor- General's Legislative Council and for legislatures in the provinces. There was also the Government of India's Act of 1919 under which provincial governments responsible to provincial legislative councils were given significant non-political power, and under which a bicameral legislature was established. Then there was the famous Government of India Act of 1935 which incorporated all the preceding stages of constitutional development, and added two new principles: That a Federal structure should be organised, and that relatively popular governments should be allowed to function in the provinces. Consider the era of the thirties when national political parties were allowed to contest the elections, and were allowed to form their own governments wherever they gained a majority in the legislature. The Indian National Congress, for example—having gained elections in all the provinces except three—were able to govern most of India at the provincial level. The task of governance thus was not limited only to the empire builders, but was extended to Indians who finally ruled India after independence. The development of self-governing institutions in India—just as the ideas of political freedom—were thus the result of a continual interaction between enlightened Englishmen and Indian public opinion. This was the great legacy that India inherited. There was Lord Richard Colley Wellesley (governor-general of India 1797-1805) who considered the administering of India as a "sacred trust"; there was Sir John Malcolm, Governor of Bombay, who insisted that "we must, or we cannot last, contrive to associate the natives with us in the task of rule, and in the benefits and gratifications which accrue from them."[33] And then there was, to take just another example, Lord Francis Rawdon-Hastings Governor- General of India during the beginning of the nineteenth century (1813) who went even further envisaging for the first time a voluntary withdrawal of British power. In a prophetic mood, he wrote in his private journal (17 May 1818):

> A time not very remote will arrive when England will on sound principles of policy wish to relinquish the domination which she has gradually and unintentionally assumed over this country, and from which it cannot at present recede. In that hour it would be the proudest boast and most delightful deflection that she had used her sovereignty towards enlightening her temporary subjects, so as to enable the native communities to walk alone in the paths of justice, and to maintain with probity their benefactress that commercial intercourse in which she should then found solid interest.[34]

These were indeed noble sentiments. But as stated above, these visions about the future of India, was not the only element that contributed to the unfolding of the process of developing self-governing institutions. There were also pressure groups among Westernised Indians who had faith in the British sense of justice and fair play, and who believed in developing self-governing institutions under the protective framework of British rule. In this group were lawyers like Motilal Nehru, W.C. Banerjee, Pherozeshah Mehta, teachers like Tilak, journalists like Motilal Ghosh and G. Subranya Iyer and administrators like R.C. Dutt and Raja Madhav Rao.

It was thus these destructive and regenerative aspects of British rule that spawned nationalism and political liberalism on the subcontinent. If it was the economic poverty, resulting from British exploitation, that led to discontent in the country, it was the British education, the European discovery of India's glorious past, and ideas of political freedom that catalysed the Indian elite to assert its own identity, and unfolded that long and tortuous process of nationalism which finally culminated in the independence of the country in 1947.

References

1. Ibid., p. 36.
2. Philip Mason, *The Men who ruled India,* London: Jonathan Cape, 1985, p. 51.
3. Ibid, p. 38-39.
4. N.K. Sinha, *The Economic History of Bengal Calcutta,* Firma K.L. Mukhpadhyay, 1961, Vol I.
5. John Keay, *The Honourable Company: A History of the East India Company,* London: Harper Collins Publishers, 1991, p. xx.
6. For details of the Company, see Antony Wild, *The East India Company-Trade and Conquest from 1600* London: Harper Collins 1955.

7. J. Pirenne, *History of the Universe,* San Fransico : Barrett-Kochler, 2002.
8. Adam Smith, *The Wealth of Nations,* London: Methuen and Co, 1904, p. 348.
9. J.B. Tavernier, *Travels in India,* London: Oxford University Press, 1889, Vol II, p. 2.
10. Ibid, p. 59.
11. Ibid., p. 75.
12. F. Bernier, *Travels in the Mogul Empire,* Delhi : Asian Educational Services, 1891, p. 227.
13. Ibid., p. 440.
14. Cited in Romesh Dutt, *The Economic History of India in the Victorian Age 1837-1900,* London : Routledge, 1960, p. VII.
15. Ibid., p. xxvi.
16. Ibid., p. xxvi.
17. G.H. Perris, *The Industrial History of Modern England,* London: Gappaher Press, 2007.
18. Adam Brooks, *The Law of Civilization and Decay,* New York : Macmillan and Co, 1985, p. 260.
19. R.P. Dutt, *India Today,* Bombay: Peoples Publishing House, 1946, p. 85.
20. Jabez T. Sutherland, "The New Nationalist Movement in India," *The Atlantic* October 1908, p. 10.
21. R.C. Dutt, op. cit.
22. W.S. Lilly, *India and its Problems,* London: Sands, 1902.
23. K. Marx and F. Engels, op. cit., p. 33.
24. Ibid., pp. 36-37.
25. Maurice and Taya Zinken, *Britain and India: Requiem for Empire, London:* Oxford University Press, 1964.
26. Ibid., p. 71.
27. Nirad C. Chaudhuri, *Thy Hand Great Anarch India 1921-1952,* London: Chatto and Windus, 1988.
28. Ibid.
29. G.O. Trevelyan, *The Life and Letters of Lord Macaulay,* Middlesex: Echo Library, 1876, pp. 329-330.

30. John Keay, *India: A History,* London: The Folio Society, 2003, p. 494.
31. Cited in R.P. Masani, *Britain in India,* London: Oxford University Press, 1960, pp.32-38.
32. Nirad C. Chaudhuri, *The Autobiography of an unknown Indian,* London : Picador, 1999, p. 425.
33. Cited in H.G. Rawlinson, *The British Achievements in India,* London: 1952, William Hodge and Co, 1948, p. 62.
34. Cited in R.P. Masani, op. cit. pp. 25-26.

2

Nationalism

The history of the present century has been marked at one and the same time by the impact of the west on Asia and Africa and by the revolt of Asia and Africa against the west

G. Barraclough 1966

The roots of Indian nationalism can be traced to two basic phenomena—the instinct of emotion and the burden of tradition. Emotion was the dislike of the foreigner, and the tradition was a deeply rooted Hinduism, which, from time immemorial, firmly believed in the fundamental unity of India.

The 11th century Arab philosopher declared that the Hindus believed "that there is no country but theirs, no nation like theirs, no religion like theirs. They are haughty, foolishly vain, self-conceited and stoled."[1]

This contempt for the outsiders, and the building up of an exaggerated image of oneself is nothing new and is almost a universal phenomenon. In India, it can be discerned through the years when it was a victim of repeated invasions. Most of the ideas, cultures and civilisations that incidentally flowed into the country in the aftermath of invasions were invariably rejected on the ground that there was nothing in them that was comparable to the ideas surrounding the Hindu thought.

This did not of course mean that the Hindus fought continuously with the foreigners, that they refused to have anything do with them, that they retired into the hills, the jungles or the desert in order to maintain a distance between themselves and the "impure" outsider. On the contrary, the history of India is full of examples of Hindus rendering all sorts of practical services to the foreigners who ruled India, particularly to the Muslims in pre-British India—services like running Muslim administrations, commanding Muslim armies, and bringing other Hindus under Muslim subjection. But beyond these things the Hindus drew a clear line. Their cultural life, their religious behaviour, their customs and their mores were considered totally different from that of the foreigner, and they had to be kept as such. During the long period of Muslim occupation, for example, Hindu lawmakers continued to tighten rules against inter-marriages and commensality. New rules were introduced to control contact with the foreigner, and the imitation of his manners. Although, as mentioned above, the Hindus were not forbidden to work for the foreigner or wear his dress when worldly interests required such a practice, the foreign customs, however, had to be discarded in the outer house, and the wearer had to purify himself by touching Ganges water before he could allow himself to enter into the inner house. One of the great Bengali novelists of the twentieth century, Sarat Chandra Chatterji, had summed up this attitude in a clear manner. In one his writings, he creates a woman, who, though having lived with a low caste paramour for twenty years, never allowed him to enter her kitchen.

The Hindu tradition was also instrumental in generating a mood of nationalism in the country. An examination of the ancient Hindu sources—as had been done by some scholars[2]—shows the dimensional contribution of Hindu religion to the growth of a geographical sense in the people, and to the development of the perception of the fundamental unity of India. Consider the famous river hymn of the Rig-Veda which englobes the whole of northern India. Consider the decision of Shankaracharya, the Hindu vedanist phiiosopher of the nineteenth century, to name the four most meritorious pilgrimages in India placed in the four extreme points of the country, so that the entire country may be known by the people and the whole area held sacred. And, consider the Pauranic couplet in which the whole of India is represented—including the South—as the land of seven rivers. "Oye." it says, "Ganga, Yamuna. Godavari, Sarasvati, Narmada, Sindhu and Kaveri, come ye and enter into this water of my offering."[3]

But this emotion and this tradition, while consensual among Hindus, were by no means a sufficient foundation for the development of a national movement; they could of course provide some meaning and some impetus, but they could not create it. They were indeed too abstract and too nebulous to spawn a coherent movement.

Clearly, within the general framework of the traditional Hindu system, there was nothing that could generate secular nationalism, and give a real meaning to this general feeling of rampant discontent. Some sort of a stimulus was evidently needed from the outside—a stimulus that was intellectual and cohesive.

This was provided by the Western world, which came, not as a challenge to a closed religious system—as was the case with Islam—but in the form of universal ideas in a secular setting, which could be accepted and even acted upon, without colliding with or undermining the Hinduist social, religious and traditional values. Unlike the early Western incursions of the Portuguese in the sixteenth century when the Western world was presented in the form of religious ideas, the Western influence through the British came into India in a secular setting.

Thousands of Indians were exposed to the English language for career purposes, and certain personalities and movements influenced many of them. The first and rational facet was indoctrinated by Edmund Burke and John Stuart Mill, but shaped in its practical expression by the liberalism of William Wart Gladstone and Abraham Lincoln. The second facet was purely emotional, and Jean Jacques Rousseau and Giuseppe Mazzini furnished its inspiration. The leaders of the American Revolution, the Italian Risorgimento—particularly Giuseppe Garibaldi—and the Irish nationalists suggested the methods of political action. The entire course of English history, and, more especially, the turmoils of the seventeenth century, together with the American, French, Italian and Irish movements were freely drawn for precedents and also for operational hints,

All these ideas and movements, slowly spreading among the Indian elite, generated an attitude of uneasiness. How can we, many of them asked, get even with this new phenomena from the West without being false to our own tradition, and is there something in the Western world which might be of value to us in reforming our own society? If physical force was no remedy against this foreign rule inflicted upon us could we not use these very ideas to mobilise ourselves and counter them? Should not rights replace canons as weapons, and should rhetoric not take the place of volleys of musketry? And how about the old Hindu customs of infanticide, superstition, rigid caste system, or the immolation of women on the funeral pyre of their husbands? Are Europeans not justified in attacking these highly irrational and objectionable aspects of Hindu society?

NEW TRENDS IN HINDUISM

All these uneasy questions, which might have passed over the head of a traditional Indian, left an indelible impression in the minds of the new group of Hindus who had increasingly become exposed to Western thought; and there thus began a process of adaptation to this new intrusion through the resurgence of new social and religious reform movements which gave a new dimension to the Hindu mind, and which constituted a significant prelude to the political awakening of the subccntinent.

One of the first architects of this new movement was Raja Ram Mohan Roy, a Bengali Brahmin, whose life and thought crystallised this whole situation and provided lines of development for the future. He combined in himself the old and the new, the religious and secular, the past and the future and the east and the west. Deeply versed in Indian thought and philosophy, a scholar of Sanskrit, Persian and Arabic, he was the product of mixed Hindu-Muslim culture that was then dominant among the upper classes. The coming of the British to India and their superiority in many ways led his curious and adventurous mind to find out their cultural roots, and to familiarise himself with the whole spectrum of ideas and influences that had cast England into a new mould. He learnt English but this was not enough; he learnt Greek, Latin, and Hebrew to discover the sources of religion and culture of the West. Science and the technical aspects of Western civilisation also attracted him, though they were not so obvious as they became subsequently.

It was this exposure to different schools of philosophical, religious and social thoughts that led Roy to underline the fundamental unity of all religions, to stress the relevance of monotheism, and to reject the dogmatic structures of all religious tradition—including his own,

But, he was not only a scholar. He was also a reformer—a reformer who fearlessly advocated the necessary changes demanded by his age. Though Islam influenced him in his early years, and later, to some extent, by Christianity, he maintained his identification with Hinduism, and attempted to reform that faith, ridding it of abuses and evil practices that had become associated with it. It was largely because of his agitation for the abolition of *suttee* that the British Government prohibited it.

Ram Mohan Roy also launched the first of the religious movements. He considered that reason, as expressed in the Upanishads were the basis of Hindu religion, and that all social institutions or customs should be judged from that standpoint. From this premise he drew two conclusions: that Hindu society needed radical reform, and that Hinduism could welcome external influences which were not contrary to the spirit of reason. Also. he considered that the recognition of human rights was consistent with basic Hindu thought, and expressed in his *Brahmo Samaj* or Divine society founded in 1830.

Elsewhere in India also the same tendencies were at work, and dissatisfaction arose at the rigid social forms and protean character of Hinduism.

Swami Dayananda Saraswati, a Brahmin, was the other spiritual leader who started one of the most notable reform movements in the second half of the nineteenth century. This was the *Arya Samaj*, and its slogan was "Back to the Vedas". These original scriptures contained all knowledge and "are the words of God".[4] From this fundamentalist basis, he denounced the later distorted accretions of Hindu society. Most of them he rejected, and produced a simple, militant and dynamic creed, which proved especially attractive to the Hindus of the Punjab. He questioned the authority of the Brahmin, and rejected infinite number of meaningless rites, casteism, idolatry, polygamy, child marriage and the seclusion of the widows. The ritual centred on the simple fire ceremony of the early Aryans, and worship became congregational. The movement was, as has been suggested by some writers, was "really the beginning of that religious and social revival amongst the Hindus of India to which we owe largely the birth of our present national consciousness."[5] But certain aggressiveness confined its main appeal to the Punjab, while its very militant and rather dogmatic character led it into intolerance towards the Muslims and Christians. Undoubtedly, *Arya Samaj* did play a crucial role in the early stages of Indian nationalism, and "represented a form of national awakening of the Indian people."[6]

Another movement was that of Ramakhrishna Paramahansa (1834-86). At first sight he seemed to be a typical medieval Hindu saint, but he inspired his vedantist follower, Swami Vivekananda, to found the Ramkhrishna mission. He preached the monism of the Advarta philosphy of the Vedanta and was convinced that only this could be the future religion of thinking humanity. For Vedanta was not only spiritual but also rational, and in harmony with scientific investigation of external reality. "This universe," he declared "has not been created by an extra-cosmic God, nor is it the work of an outside genius. It is self-creating, self-dissolving, self-manifesting. One infinite existence, the Brahma."[7] But in addition to this monistic existence, Vivekananda added the gospel of action to that of contemplation thus awakening the Hindus from their slumbers. Addressing the Indian youth, he said, "India is to be saved by the Indians themselves. You have been told that you can do nothing, and nonentities you are becoming every day. What we want is strength. So believe yourself.... Make your nerves strong. What we want is muscles of iron and nerves of steel."[8] He told the Indians that the east was deep in wisdom and rich in spiritual values, and exhorted them that they should conquer the spiritually shallow West, through their philosophy and superiority of thought. By his teachings, Vivekananda created among the people a sense of confidence and self-reliance—virtues that were being overshadowed by Western learning, science and technology. His was a great contribution to the awakening of India.

Theosophy was another religiously oriented reform movement that was started in India under the impact of new Indian and international conditions. The uniqueness of the movement consisted in the fact that a non-Indian who was a great admirer of Hinduism inaugurated it. Theosophy subscribed to the spiritual philosophy of ancient Hinduism, preached the universal brotherhood of men, and proclaimed the value of Indian thought and the priceless heritage of Indian people. "The needs of India," wrote Annie Besant, the leader of the movement, "are, among others, the development of national spirit, an education founded on Indian ideals, and enriched, not dominated, by the thought and culture of the west".[9]

All of these movements, and many others, thus contributed in different ways to the awakening of India in the nineteenth century. Responding to the rapidly changing Indian reality, the reformist leaders had transplanted on Hinduism a host of European ideas that had wafted into the subcontinent. But all of them were circumscribed in their nationalistic activities by number of factors. In the first place, they did not go beyond the Hindu framework. All of them stood for the revision of traditional religions, and none of them challenged or repudiated their basic faith in Hinduism. That this preoccupation with religion was a limiting factor is evident from the fact that none of these movements were really able to constitute themselves into a real nationalist force. Second, none of these ideas and movements really generated any dimensional mass movement. The *Brahmo Samaj* was too eclectic; the *Arya Samaj* too narrow in conception, the Ramakhrishna Mission too occupied in carrying its mission to the west or too absorbed with the spiritual life of the individual, while the theosophical society had a social base that was too narrow.

It was only after the emergence of new social groups—rendered unavoidable with the increasing industrialisation of the country and the spread of education—that the linkage between religion and politics was broken. Nationalism slowly began to acquire a more secular character, without of course completely abandoning the element of religiosity that pervades much of Hindu life.

Emergence of Modern Nationalism

Indian nationalism went through a number of different phases. Initially it manifested itself like a gentle breeze, but later, through the years, it developed into a mighty force that engulfed the whole of the subcontinent.

Examining the whole century of Indian nationalism, one can discern a pattern through which it was nurtured, developed and ideologically oriented. There was initially, in the middle of the nineteenth century (1857), a violent and xenophobic defence of the existing order—an order that was in the process of being slowly destroyed by the British. A little later there was a curious swing in the opposite direction—in the direction of an uncritical self-humiliation and acceptance of alien superiority. The third stage was the emergence of new leadership of liberal tendencies with middle class participation—a change not inappropriately described by Marxist historiography as "bourgeois nationalism". Finally, there was the broadening of the base of resistance by the organisation of a mass following among peasants and workers, and the forging of a new type.[10]

The First Phase: Proto-nationalism

The first phase opened in the second quarter of the nineteenth century. It was a tumultuous period –a period of conflict between the old and the new, and between the conservative section of the Indian society and the modernising zeal of the British conquerors. After years of tussle, and the expansion of British influence over India, the exhausted country appeared to be ready to accept another foreign rule on the condition that the traditional socio-religious fabric of society, both Hindu and Muslim, was left untouched. In general the Mughals had done this, and had thus been able to extend their authority both in range and in depth without arousing any popular reaction. Besides, even if they wanted to, they had really nothing much to offer.

The British however were different. They were determined to change India and had much to offer. Equipped with new developed economic and political structures, and armed with new and secular ideas, they introduced, with great fervour, Western education and learning, permitted the Christian missionaries to propagate their religious thought, introduced Western material techniques and instruments, and allowed the introduction of the English language in institutions of higher education. The new was thus being introduced.

Most Indians, who were still hanging on to their traditional ways, considered all this as patronage, and the government was no longer associated with the idea of neutral authority but with the idea of innovation. As this impression spread, a feeling of unease and a feeling of a generalised threat to the traditional way of living began to take shape. The Christian missionaries, who showered venomous abuse on the Hindus and on their social organisms, were perceived to be voicing the views of the British authorities. Innovations like the telegraph were thought to be evil, and Western education was considered to be sowing doubts in the minds of the Indian youth about Hindu orthodoxy.

To these were added more concrete grievances. There were the great land settlements that deprived the landholders of their possessions. There was the Bombay Commission that was appointed to investigate titles of owners that confiscated some 20,000 estates.

The Indian society thus by 1850 had entered a period of stress. Tensions grew rapidly. Rumblings of discontent became more and more visible. In normal times, this process might have been kept under control until tensions had eased with the growth of understanding, and with the emergence of new classes committed to the British era in India. But, before all this could happen, tensions were brought to a focus by the activities of the new Governor- General, the

Marquees of Dalhousie (1848-56). As a convinced westerner, he vigorously pushed forward public works, planned the Indian railway system, introduced telegraphs, and organised the first three Indian universities. That these were solid achievements, of this there is no doubt; but they were all a part of the growing acculturation process that tended to aggravate the feeling of restiveness in the country.

All these bold initiatives were capped by Dalhousie's most spectacular measure—the measure to annex most of India. Within a period of eight years he seized eight large kingdoms or states. Though the overall argumentation, provided for their annexations, was Dalhousie's firm conviction that "British rule was for the benefit of the inhabitants,"[11] there were nonetheless specific reasons advanced for each military initiative. The Punjab was annexed because there was an uprising in the country. Lower Burma (Mynamar) was taken over on the complaints of British merchants. Berar was brutally conquered because the head of the State could not pay his debts, Satara, Jhansi and Nagpur were annexed because Dalhousie refused to recognise the heirs nominated by the rulers of these States.

The effect of all these dynastic and territorial expropriations was that they left a large number of princes landowners deeply aggrieved. The annexation of Oudh for misgovernment was perhaps the most damaging of them all since it was the most unpopular and since it aroused even the anger of many Indian soldiers. The whole affair of the takeover of Oudh was indeed indefensible and perhaps most objectionable, for few people of the kingdom "could really understand why their weak harmless prince, who had done the British no injury, but like his ancestors, had even been faithful to them, should be thrust aside. He was not a cruel tyrant and his self-indulgence and careless neglect of his subjects' welfare were not in their eyes, such heinous offences as they were to the British."[12]

Not many historians have defended Dalhousie's policies and actions on the ground of justice. They can hardly be. But, one of the most thoughtful British historian of the Victorian age, J.R. Seeley, had[13] condoned his actions by comparing them with the military actions of Frederick the Great of Prussia. But, this is hardly appropriate. Frederick's wars were against his equals, and his actions were almost redeemed by the high purpose of making his country amongst the great nations of Europe. Dalhousie, on the other hand, struck those who could not resist, and was galvanised by the mercenary objectives of building a vast empire and augmenting the revenues of East India Company.

The effect of all these dynastic and territorial expropriations was that they left a large number of princes and landowners deeply aggrieved. The annexation of Oudh for misgovernment was perhaps the most damaging of them all since it was the most unpopular, and since it aroused even the anger of many Indian soldiers. Thus, when Dalhousie left India in 1856 the apparent public tranquillity concealed a tense situation that was waiting for an incident to provide the necessary explosion.

The military authorities provided the incident. The total insensibility of the British Army officers to religious susceptibilities of the Hindus and Muslim sepoys led them to introduce a particular species of cartridge—unclean for both religions—for the new Enfield rifle which was greased with lard made from the fat of either the hog or the ox. All available evidence indicates that it had terrible repercussions on the sepoys scattered all over the country. The story spread like a wildfire, generating excitement and consternation all over the sepoy world. There is no doubt that letters to this effect were exchanged between soldiers widely separated in localities far distant from each other. Many of these letters intercepted by the Government indicated the rampancy of a strong belief among the soldiers that it was a deliberate device to destroy their religious beliefs, and of a widespread determination to resist any such efforts even at the cost of their lives. That this incident worked as a spark to the already heap of powder magazine of dissatisfaction and resentment is evident from the train of events that escalatingly followed one another leading to the 1857 uprising. On 29th March, Mangal Panday, a Brahmin Sepoy, stationed at Barrackpur openly mutinied and called upon his comrades "to join him to defend and die for their religion and caste."[14] Similar incidents were repeated in Ambala and Lucknow. In Meerut, after the imprisonment of eighty five soldiers who had refused to touch the cartridges on the parade ground, the troops raised the flag of revolt, forced the release of their comrades, indiscriminately shot their officers, committed acts of indescribable horror on European families and marched towards Delhi. There in that imperial city, the Mughul Emperor, Bahadur Shah as the Emperor of India, was persuaded to assume their leadership. The development of these dramatic events created a great sensation all over northern India where the soldiers rebelled massively and where the disgruntled princes and chieftains assumed their leadership. Inevitably the fever of excitement and revolt spread to the civilian population. The Hindus and Muslims, the higher and lower classes, the landowners and the farmers, all saw in the uprising an opportunity of avenging the wrongs done to them by the British. It appeared as though the revolt would escalate into a real war of independence making the British re-conquest almost impossible. But by September the situation changed—in fact radically. The "mutiny" could not maintain any momentum, and rapidly began to loose strength. The Indian rebels, in the first place, were not able to work upon some settled plan under one national leader. Second, the bond of unity that apparently appeared to be quite strong between the Hindus and Muslims and between the sepoys and the civilian population in the initial stages was really not solid; for evidence increasingly began to emerge that real communal amity was missing, and that many of the civilians who had suffered at the hands of the sepoys sincerely hoped for the early restoration of British rule. The strength of the rebels began to shatter and their prestige began to wane. Slowly the British were successful in overpowering the forces of rebellion everywhere.

What was the dimension of such an upheaval? Was it one of the passing episodes of Indian history which has left hardly any imprint on the country, or has it acquired the pride of place in the history of Indian nationalism? And from the maze of events that surround the revolt can one really discern the presence of clear-cut objectives of those social groups that were actively involved?

Opinions differ among historians. While there are some who appear to question the national dimension of the event,[15] there are others who regard it as the "national war of independence,"[16] which was "the first combined attempt of many classes of people to challenge the foreign power."[17]

But these divergences do not seem to extend to the underlying motives that instigated the different groups to participate in the upheaval. Most of the historians seem to agree to the "proto-nationalist" character of the revolt, and to the lack of any real national coherence. The princes strove for the reversion of their domains seized by the British, the feudal lords struggled for the re-establishment of the same disunited feudal India of the pre-British days, and the religious leaders were aiming at the restoration of traditional India unaffected by the winds of secular ideas that had wafted the subcontinent.

However, despite its limited dimension, and its traditional character, the effect of this major event both on the British as well as the Indians was considerable.

On the British side it exercised a tremendous influence upon the British policy in India. The cruelties perpetrated by the rebels upon the English men women and children were remembered with deep hatred for many years The revolt of the Brahmins particularly shocked them, for they had been the most-favoured of all sepoys, and their religious privileges had been safeguarded at the expense of military efficiency. The

English became distrustful of the Indians, above all of the high-caste Hindus.

The end of the "Mutiny" therefore resulted in the inauguration of a new policy the purpose of which was to strengthen British hold over India. One of the first momentous acts carried out was the extinction of the East India Company's rule and the assumption of direct government by the British crown. Although such a trend was already discernible before the events, the whole process was accelerated after 1857. Clearly, East India Company had lost all credibility of administering the subcontinent leaving no other alternative for the British Government but to directly take over the country. The Indian army, furthermore, was reorganised. The proportion of British soldiers was increased, the different classes of sepoys, hitherto separated from each other for religious and social reasons, were mixed, and effective weapons of warfare were no longer entrusted to the Indians; even the most experienced non-commissioned Indian officer was now given a status inferior to that of a raw English subaltern. The British Government abandoned the Company's policy of liquidating the native States and converting the entire subcontinent into British territory. While all steps were taken to weaken them militarily, a new policy of seeking conciliation with the ruling families and transforming them into allies was inaugurated. That this was a major innovation is evident from the fact that most of the native States, essentially feudal in character, were unaffected by winds of change introduced by the British and became strongholds of real conservatism and reaction. The heavy loss of life also made the British wary of continuing their politics of occidentalisation. It was realised that the 1857 uprising was partly due to the innovating policies of Dalhousie and to the legislation that affected social life. The next eighty years were therefore marked by an unwillingness to interfere with religious and caste issues. "The Indian Government's honeymoon with progress," confirmed Percival Spear, "was over and was to be followed by the humdrum process of getting along with traditionalist partner."[18] The British realised that it was their responsibility to keep peace and maintain law and order, but not to worry about Indian family structures or private morals. They adopted in the post-mutiny period a policy of neutrality on all religious and social questions.

The effect of the "mutiny" on the Indians was also profound. The success of the tiny British force in quelling such a widespread revolt led many Indians to question the effectiveness of armed resistance, and encouraged many of them to seek alternative methods of expressing their discontent. That this was a significant development is evident from the fact that never again did armed resistance occupy a central place in India's subsequent history. There were of course occasional armed uprisings like the Wahabis, a militant Muslim sect, in the North West Frontier Province, the Maharattas in Bombay and the indigo cultivators in Bengal, but none of them were strong enough to challenge British hold over India. The last embers of confusion, chaos and violence had been finally extinguished and a new era had begun in Indian history. Furthermore, as the dust began to settle, it gradually became clear that the country was turning away from the traditional leaders, and was showing signs of serious doubts regarding the adequacy of traditional beliefs and institutions. As a corollary, it began to turn, without openly admitting it, to the new emerging Europeanised class. While the traditional chiefs remained decorative emblems enjoying much outward respect, hope for the future were more and more pinned on new leaders exposed to Western culture. The evidence of this silent but nonetheless fundamental shift in orientation is to be found in the sudden upsurge of English education. Originally, the government and the missionaries had set the pace, but now after the mutiny it was taken over by the nascent middle class who—conscious and impressed by the Western model—felt that the country's salvation reposed on adopting it. The new attitude undoubtedly played a role in giving a new form to Indian aspirations. But it was not only the intellectual ferment that acted as a real catalyst to the birth of political consciousness and to the appearance on the horizon of a new sense of nationalism, though it was certainly there as the backdrop; It was really the emergence of discontent that gave the country a new momentum—a discontent caused by the degenerating economic situation and repressive British measures.

In the post-mutiny aftermath the heavy burden of land revenue and rents was increasingly felt by the peasants, the quantum of famines had amplified resulting in an estimated total of over twenty eight million deaths, and the handicraft industries, the linchpin of pre-industrial economy, had declined seriously. The harsh and oppressive measures under Lord Lytton's administration had an adverse effect on political life in India. The Vernacular Press Act of 1878 had restricted the freedom of the press, the abolition of import duties on cotton discriminated against the Indian textile industry, and the age reduction—from 21 to 19—for candidates appearing for the civil service examinations made it difficult for young Indians to compete for careers in the administrative service.

The level of discontent took a turn for the worse with the introduction of Ripon's ILBERT bill—a bill that was expected to provide equal treatment to the Europeans, and the Indians in the field of criminal jurisdiction. The entire European community, fearful of the threat it constituted to its privileged status, organised a powerful and fierce agitation against the bill. A plot was hatched "to put the Viceroy on board a steamer at Chandpat Ghat and send him to England via the Cape."[19] On the other hand, the Indians, who perceived the bill as a welcome step, were incensed by its defeat thus exacerbating the tensions between the Europeans and Indians.

The cumulative effect of all these factors was the opening of a new era of intense political agitation the dimension of which was really national. But, both the form as well as the content of this nationalist swagger was different from the pre-Mutiny days in so far as it was peaceful, and in so far as the objectives were no longer the safeguarding of traditional structures. The new middle class consensus was that the salvation of the country lay in the adoption of the European model.

The agitation took the form of considerable rhetoric in the Indian press against the harsh and repressive measures imposed by the Government. Trenchant remarks were made even on such subjects as the Afghan War, the military expedition to Egypt, and the favouritism shown to Manchester at the cost of the rate payers. Mass political meetings were held all over the country, political centres with branches in districts were organised, memorials and petitions to the government were signed massively, and efforts were made to educate public opinion in England, and arouse its interest in Indian affairs. India, according to one writer, was "brought under Lord Lytton with measurable distance of a revolutionary outbreak."[20]

In the view of some British liberals, something had to be done before the new and already threatening situation took a dangerous turn engulfing India in chaos and confusion. The traumatic experience of the Mutiny—still rankling in the minds of many—had to be avoided.

It was this realisation that prompted a British Liberal, Allan Octavian Hume, who had a strategic position in the Home Department, to persuade Lord Dufferin, then the Viceroy of India, to create a national organisation which could serve as a focal point for national discontent, especially of the educated classes, and guide the discontent in channels of constitutional movement for political advancement. In short "a safety valve for the escape of great and growing forces"[21] was urgently needed.

With the active encouragement from the Viceroy, Hume now dedicated himself to the important task of creating a national organisation, which was finally established in 1885.

The creation of the new national organisation—the Indian National Congress—was undoubtedly an important landmark in the history of Indian nationalism inaugurating a new phase which can be characterised as "uncritical self-humiliation and acceptance of alien superiority."[22]

Second Phase: Imitative Nationalism

The original leaders, who shaped the programme of the Congress Party during the first two phase of its existence (1885-1905), were principally lawyers, teachers and administrators. Coming from the upper strata of the Indian society, and being a product of Western education, they had developed an unequivocal faith in the British sense of justice and fairplay, and believed that India's linkage with the West through England was a boon rather than a curse. "She, Britain," argued W.C. Bannerjee at the inaugural meeting of the party, "had given them (to Indians) order, She had given them railways, and, above all, She had given them the inestimable blessing of Western education."[23] Their desire to be governed according to ideas prevalent in Europe was in a way incompatible with their loyalty to the British Government. Their grievance, if any, was in the slowness of British applicability of their own ideas onto India. The entire spectrum of their political activity was therefore limited to the achievement of such goals as the widening of the basis of the Government, the separation of the judicial and executive functions, the indianisation of services, the resuscitation of the declining handicraft industry, the stoppage of the economic drain which engendered the poverty of the Indian people, the protection of Indian industries and the repeal of repressive acts.

Other liberal leaders also articulated similar views. There was Dadabhai Naoroji who spoke of "self-government or Swaraj like that of the United Kingdom."[24] There was Pherozeshah Mehta who expressed "unbounded faith in the living and fertilising principles of English culture and English civilisation;"[25] and there was Sardar Dayal Singh Majithia, Chairman of the Congress reception committee who called the party in 1893 "as the greatest glory of British rule in this country."[26]

The most striking example of this group, however, was the Maratha Brahmin, Gopal Krishna Gokhale. Like other Congress leaders of the period, he accepted British rule as "the inscrutable dispensation of providence" and asked for greater liberalism in practice and a larger share in the government for educated Indians. True to his ideas he worked closely with the British Government often playing the thankless role of interpreting the Indian people to the British and the British administration to the Indians. He served on the Indian Legislative Council for years and won the respect and friendship of Lord Curzon himself. However, despite his success as a parliamentarian. Gokhale lacked the attributes of a popular leader. His political activities were focussed on the Council Chamber rather than the village square; and he had "the remarkable knack of saying the hardest thing in the gentlest language."[27]

Imitative nationalism, arguably, may seem contradiction in terms. But it is not. For, while this group was impressed by the vitality of the British system, and its appropriateness as a role model, they were nonetheless nationalistic enough to advance the idea of wider Indian participation in the affairs of the

State. Clearly the concept of nationalism of those days had dual characteristics. On the one hand it was weak because it was restricted in composition and numbers. They had become rootless with no reach to the people and no understanding of what they wanted. In many ways they were less connected to the country than the ones who led the "mutiny", since the population could recognise in and identify with the harsh rhetoric of the traditionalist leaders. But, on the other hand, they were the avatars of progress for they had laid down the ideological basis of what linchpinned political democracy. But, imitative nationalism finally became less impactful not so much in ideas as in the limited numbers it represented. The small in numbers outweighed the bigness of ideas, and were sidelined by history and new developments. And finally liberal reforms under British over lordship were no longer considered sufficient, and were no longer acceptable to the middle class of changing India—a middle class that was expanding rapidly.

A number of reasons had catapulted this new thinking in Indian politics. There was of course the continued British indifference to the declining economic situation of the people, and to their clear opposition to the moderate demands of the Congress Party; there was the miserable plight of the Indians in South Africa who could not even walk on footpaths, could not travel in first and second class railway compartments, could not possess native gold, could not go to certain hospitals, hotels and schools, and were often spat upon, hissed, cursed, abused and subjected to a variety of other indignities; the echoes of all these humiliations was reverberating in India for which the British were openly blamed since they were the ones who had encouraged Indians to migrate to South Africa as contractual labourers. There was also the remarkable victory of Asian Japan over European Russia in 1905 that amply proved to the Indians the vincibility of the Europeans. This was an emotional reaction which was far less powerful in generating a broad feeling of indianness.

All these factors were obviously important. And all of them cumulatively contributed to the broadening of the base of Indian nationalism. But, the most important factor that really "completed the breach between a slow-moving government and politically conscious Indians"[28] were the reactionary policies of Curzon. A romantic and brilliant aristocrat, touched with late Victorian imperialism, he had a meteoric rise. From a promising but nonetheless junior government position, he became the Viceroy of India—a country he regarded as "the brightest gem in the British crown of Empire, but as a gem of antique and somewhat barbaric lustre which a modern setting could only spoil."[29] He completely overhauled the administrative structure, reduced the number of elected members of the Calcutta Corporation to half, detached the north-western district from the Punjab to form a new province supervised directly by the Government of India, brought university educational system under the firm control of the Government, and encouraged the employment of Eurasians and Christians to the police service at the expense of other Indian communities. But, the element that sparked agitational politics was Curzon's decision to partition Bengal in 1905. Bengal was an overgrown province of 78 million comprising Bengal, Bihar and Orissa. Its division had long been discussed but Curzon's contribution was to take a tidy decision where others had only talked. He created a new province of East Bengal and of Assam of 31 million people with its capital at Dhaka. It was probably more than a coincidence that East Bengal was mainly Muslim while the West was Hindu with Bengalis as a minority amongst Biharis and Oriyas.

The partition sparked massive agitation. No British statesman had served the cause of Indian nationalism more than Curzon had. "He (Curzon) has," opined Surendranath Banerjee, "built better than he knew; he has laid broad and deep the foundations of our national life; he has stimulated these forces which contribute to the upbuilding of nations; he has made us a nation; and the most reactionary of Viceroys will go down to posterity as the architect of the Indian national life.[30]"

Third Phase: Bourgeois Nationalism

The effect of all these measures was that it spawned a new spirit—a spirit of revolt against the politics of liberalism and of constitutional methods followed by Gokhale. The new leaders advocated agitation and mass action. They had lost all faith in the efficacy of constitutional approach, for this, they believed, could bear fruit only in a democracy where the government was responsible to the people, which was clearly not the case with India. Piecemeal reforms were of no avail, and that ending, not mending, the British rule, was the only option available for the country.

But, this militant nationalism was expressed in religious terms. It was clothed in religio-mystical form. The Vedic past of the Hindus was constantly evoked, the reigns of Ashoka and Chandragupta were projected as the role-models, the heroic deeds of Rana Pratap and Shivaji, were placed on the roster of historic personalities, while the epic patriotism of Laxmibai (the Queen of Jhansi) during the 1857 revolt, was proffered as the inspirational examples for the people of India. Clearly the new militant leaders were well versed in ancient learning and ancient thought, and were deeply religious. For Aurobindo Ghosh in Bengal "nationalism is a religion that has come from God;"[31] for Lajpat Rai in Punjab, nationalism had to be raised "to the level of religion;"[32] while Tilak in Maharashtra declared that a linkage had to be established between nationalism and religion.[33]

Since the militant nationalists considered British and Indian interests as irreconcilable, they rejected the limited political reform movement conceived by the Indian liberals during the early phase. The liberal goals of obtaining administrative reforms, of indianising the services, of seeking governmental assistance to resuscitate the declining handicraft industry were no longer perceived as sufficient to meet the rising national aspirations of the country. Nothing short of real political independence, in their view, could satisfy the nation, or make it possible for them to accomplish basic socio-economic programmes.

The militants also rejected the moderate forms of constitutional agitation that the Indian liberals had programmed; for it did not have, in their view, any great usefulness in a country ruled autocratically by a foreign nation. In its stead they proposed a comprehensive programme which included, among other things, the boycotting of British goods, the renunciation of titles and government posts, and non-participating in Legislative Councils and educational institutions set up by the authorities. Targeting specifically the British, some of the leaders argued that "the logic of losing business is more likely to impress the nation of shopkeepers than any argument based on the ethics of justice."[34]

India thus was never the same again. The whole of the middle class, and in Bengal the people as a whole had been deeply stirred. Broadly the result was the capture of this class by a revivified Congress Party. Nationalism, which had hitherto been the opinion and the aspiration of the more active members of the class, had become their settled conviction and instinctive attitude of all of them. The pains of the Bengal partition were the birth pangs of bourgeois nationalism.

But there were other results as well of this new middle class nationalism. It became evident that the bourgeoisie might on occasion get a popular backing, that the old aristocratic leaders could not any more restrain than they could lead the people, that action could indeed follow rhetoric.

All these sentiments and the new upsurge of nationalism gave a new dimension to the nature of new agitation. Country-wide campaigns to boycott British goods were successfully organised, mass meetings were held, demonstrations were staged, and the new nationalist press sprang up to begin an organised campaign to educate the people in the new outlook and the new programme.

The climax of this new form of agitation was a split within the Congress Party in 1907 at Surat. Tilak and his followers, representing the radical nationalist wing of the party, insisted on the drafting of resolutions stressing self-government, national education and the use of boycott as a major instrument against the British; but a furious melee on the floor of the Surat meeting resulted in the victory of the conservative wing of the party whereupon Tilak and his followers walked out of the congress party.

But this departure from the party did not eclipse Tilak; he did not disappear in the limbo of oblivion; for he rapidly organised an intensive campaign and a furious broadside against the British that led to his arrest and imprisonment for 6 years in Mandalay. Finally he returned to the Congress Party as its undisputed leader where he remained as the central force until his death in 1920.

Tilak's appearance on the Indian political scene marked a new stage in the history of Indian nationalism. The original spectacle that the Indian leadership had hitherto projected of a polite debating society, accepting British values and British ideals, had been firmly rejected. And in its stead was introduced the new goal of national independence to be achieved through agitational politics. But this new pattern of radical political behaviour acquired a specific form—a form specially directed at Hindu mobilisation through an intense revivalist campaign that included organising celebrations and processions of the elephant-headed God, Ganesh, of resuscitating the memory of Shivaji, the chieftain who had originally established himself through his battles against the Mughals.

But this new stage in Indian nationalism—though undoubtedly important—still had a relatively a narrow middle class base with disaffected students as the major spearhead. Through its agitational politics it had shaken British rule but not enough to push the British to make concessions to share power with the Indians. Something more massive was clearly needed to make Indian nationalism more impactful and more weighty. This was provided by nationalism entering a new phase—a phase of mass nationalism.

Fourth Phase: Mass and Militant Nationalism

But all this underwent a sea change after World War I, for there appeared on the political horizon a new man of consequence with a new dimension. He was Mohandas Karamchand Gandhi. This remarkable man, born in Porbander in a small State of Kathiawar in 1869, was a perfect representative of the masses of Indian. In the long and painful history of their existence, the masses have had many prophets to preach their ethos and voice their idealistic aspirations, but none who so completely was their own. He remained theirs even after birth and education had done practically everything to bring about a separation. Neither his station in life nor his legal education in England, nor even the western intellectual atmosphere, to which he was exposed, succeeded in making him understand the esoteric things of the intellect. He truly represented the traditional, self-mortifying and beggarly asceticism of India, and lived in utter nakedness of spirit till his death. For a sophisticated and European oriented intellectual like Jawaharlal Nehru, Gandhi was "like a powerful current of fresh air", which "made us stretch ourselves and take deep breaths; like a beam of light that pierced the darkness and removed the scales from our eyes; like a whirlwind that upset many things but most of all the working of people's mind. He did not descend from the top; he seemed to emerge from the millions of India, speaking their language and incessantly drawing attention to them and their appalling condition."[35]

One of his first most remarkable and striking contribution was the spawning of a psychological revolution that transformed the behaviour of many people. In his quiet, but nonetheless determined manner he succeeded in making people become less fearful of the British, more confident about themselves, their past and even their future. He persuaded them to abandon their traditional pacifism and adopt a fighting attitude; and he convinced the middle classes to abandon their idea of imitative politics of limiting their action to the legislative chamber or to their own class, but to go to the villages to establish an important linkage with the masses—a linkage which gives a democratic character to politics.

But it was not only in the sphere of behaviour and perceptions that he was instrumental in bringing about a transformation among the people. It was also in the field of restructuring his party that his role became decisive.

When he assumed the leadership of the party, it was given the character of a mass organisation. The peasants joined the party, and the new organisation began to assume the look of a vast agrarian structure defending the rights and interests of those who had hitherto ignored the movement. The leadership too was transformed. Though it still emanated from the well-to-do middle class, it was given a new dimension and a new purpose. "He sent us to the villages", wrote Nehru, "and the countryside hummed with the activity of innumerable messengers of the new gospel of action. The peasant was shaken up and he began to emerge from his quiescent shell. The effect on us was different but equally far-reaching, for we saw for the first time as it were, the village in the intimacy of his mud hut, and with the stark shadow of hunger always pursuing him. We learnt our Indian economics more from these visits than from books and learned discourses. The emotional experience we had had already undergone was emphasised and confirmed, and henceforth there could be no going back for us to our old life or our old standards, howsoever much pure views might change subsequently."[36]

The organisational structure of the party was also transformed. It became an organisation with weighty links from the village to the district and province and thence to the top. Such a structure made it possible to mobilise the masses, to be kept informed of the desires and the wishes of the people, and to rapidly and effectively inform the rank and file of any changes that were brought about at the top. All this was vital, for no movement can thrive, or develop a mass base without an effectively established organisational network.

The objectives of the party also changed. In fact they were heavily mutated. Under Gandhi's leadership the former goal of "self-government within the British Empire" was replaced by a more audacious goal of complete independence, although it was understood that it would accept Dominion Status or independence within the British Commonwealth.

The weapon that was adopted to carry out the nationalist struggle against the British contained a typical Indian garb—the garb of non-violence and non-cooperation. It was an echo from the ancient Hindu practice of so-called "sitting dharna," a practice whereby a creditor or an aggrieved person sat at the doorstep of his debtor or oppressor and fasted until death or until he received redress. The virtue of the practice lay in the fact that it inflicted no physical injury on the wrongdoer but only on the aggrieved.

This old form of individual struggle was given concrete form around September 1906 when Gandhi first advocated it to the Indian settlers in South Africa to protest against the Asiatic Law Amendment Bill which subjected Asians to many humiliating restrictions and requirements. To Gandhi it had the dual virtue of teaching his countrymen to shed fear and master hate.

When the Law became operational, an organisation known as the Passive Resistance Movement was formed to offer civil disobedience. It was the first demonstration of the kind, that gave considerable moral muscle to the movement. Gandhi was sentenced to two month's of imprisonment, while some of his associates were given 6 months of hard labour.

This non-violent resistance movement was given a new quantitative and qualitative dimension by Gandhi on his return from South Africa; quantitative in so far as the quantum of people offering such resistance was greatly enlarged, making it difficult for the government to withstand this massive onslaught of numbers; how could they when one takes into account the basic fact that the British in India numbered scarcely more than

300,000 out of a population of 334 million. To this was added a new qualitative element—the element of boycott of British institutions, education and goods. A detailed programme to this effect was designed on 20 March 1920 under which the entire Indian population was called upon to surrender any titles they may have obtained from the British, to give up all the honorary positions they may have been given by the colonialists, to refuse to attend official and unofficial functions held by the government, to withdraw their children from British schools and universities and send them to national institutions, to boycott courts, to refuse to offer themselves as recruits to the army, and to abstain from buying any foreign goods, particularly those emanating from Great Britain. But this was not the only original element that was injected into the nationalist movement; there were other original aspects introduced by Gandhi. He dramatised his ideas by a constant stream of articles, speeches and declarations, and above all by setting his own example i.e. by doing himself what he preached. Every reform he proposed, every advice he gave to others, he straightaway applied to himself. The simple garb that enveloped his frail body, the spinning wheel that met his clothing needs, the weekly day of silence that gave him peace, the fasts that were undertaken to dramatise his protest against British actions— all of them were emblematic signs of projecting and identifying himself with the illiterate masses. These were not sophisticated ways, but ways that made an immediate and powerful impact on the ordinary man—an impact that Gandhi was one of them.

Another facet of Gandhi's genius was his remarkable power as a popular psychologist. He dramatised himself as well as the issues he believed in. When others called meetings of protest against the objectionable bills passed by the government, Gandhi called a Hartal or a strike. When others walked out of the Legislative Chambers as a gesture of defiance, he walked two hundred miles to the sea to make illicit salt. In all that he did, he not only brought the issue in question vividly before his people, but strove to make them feel morally superior to their physically strong opponents.

One of the other major characteristic feature of Gandhi's impact on the national movement was his remarkable capacity of reconciling and holding together the many disparate groups that composed the Congress Party, thereby giving to it a character of a movement rather than a rigid political party There were socialists led by Jawaharlal Nehru who were combating right wing elements, there were people around Vallabhai Patel who were proponents of capitalism, there were orthodox Hindus who were opposed to any form of modernisation that would undermine the traditional character of Indian life. All of them Gandhi succeeded in keeping under one common platform. Undoubtedly this was one of his remarkable achievements, for successfully keeping them under one umbrella; he was able to maintain the mass character of the Indian nationalist movement.

Thus under the leadership of this fragile man— apparently the reverse of a man of action— nationalism was ramped up into a powerful movement that continuously demonstrated its capacity of mobilisation within the broad framework that Gandhi had established. There was that first major non-cooperation movement launched in 1921 to protest against the bloody Jallianwala massacre in the Punjab in 1919, and to settle the issue of the Islamic caliphate in a way acceptable to the Indian Muslims. There was his famous march to the sea in 1930 to make a handful of salt out of the sea water in order to protest against the salt tax which fell too heavily on the poor population. Immense multitudes walked with him in good order and without violence. More than 100,000 people were imprisoned and there was a general paralysis of the British administration. There was a massive campaign of non-violent protest in 1940 against the British Government's decision to declare war against Nazi Germany and Japan on behalf of India. Thousands were arrested as they tried to launch the campaign. And finally there was the landmark "quit India" campaign in August 1942. The British were asked to withdraw from India on pain of a new massive civil disobedience that was expected to coincide with the Japanese advance in the autumn of 1942. But before the movement could be actually launched, the leaders were summarily arrested. This set the spark. In the absence of the leaders and in the absence of clear lead as to the actual line of coherent action, the people did what they could or what they thought would paralyse the administration. In almost all the provinces and in a large number of princely states, there were myriad demonstrations in spite of the official ban. There were hartals, closure of shops and markets, and a stoppage of business everywhere varying in duration from a number of days to some weeks, and in some cases, to over a month. Labour also went on strike. More organised, and more used to discipline group action, industrial workers spontaneously declared strikes in many centres against government of arresting national leaders. An important example of this was in the steel city of Jamshedpur where skilled workers, drawn from all over India, kept away from work for a fortnight, and only agreed to return on a promise from the management that it would try its best to get the Congress leaders released and a national government formed. In the great textile centre of Ahmedabad there was also a sudden and complete stoppage of work in all the factories without any special call from the trade unions.

There was also violence in the country. Communications were disrupted, electric and telephone wires were cut, police stations were raided and burnt, railway carriages were attacked and put on fire; even military vehicles were destroyed. Teachers and students boycotted schools and universities, and many of them were closed. Also, there was mob violence, lawlessness, riots and disorder in certain places. In short the country was on a rampage.

What was the British reaction to this ongoing, resurgent and massive nationalism that continued to expand ceaselessly? How did they handle it? Did they, through the years, accept its growing influence, and try to reach some understanding with it, or were they immune to the nationalist aspirations of the Indians?

The immediate British response to any upheaval naturally was to control it. It could hardly be otherwise, since any let up would have seriously jeopardised the very existence of colonial rule. On every occasion, therefore, when the civil disobedience movement was launched and when the crisis simmered into an explosion, the British attitude was to arrest nationalist leaders, to firmly suppress agitations and demonstrations. But, though sometimes it was done with great brutality, often the suppression, though firm, was restrained with nationalist leaders treated kindly and even arrested with great courtesy. Those who were imprisoned—at least the political leaders—were entitled to maintain contact with the outside world, receive visitors, mingle among other fellow prisoners, and even receive food from the outside. Gandhi used to write myriad letters practically every day. Comparing his prison term in India in the thirties with what he had to go through in South Africa, he declared about his imprisonment in India, "Jail for us is no jail at all...As for me I have not felt the severity of jail life at all."[37] But, British colonialism can hardly be reduced to the simple suppression of the ongoing nationalist discontent. It had other more positive characteristics—the characteristic of establishing more benign political atmosphere on the subcontinent, on putting Indian traditionalism on the defensive, and of tolerating minimal freedom of movement, expression and organisation. But even more significant than all this is that British colonialism will also be remembered for its commitment to establish a process of institutionalising the delegation of power to Indians, and of initiating reforms that would loosen their own hold on the subcontinent.

The Indian history of the 20th century is full of myriad examples of British political reforms to appease nationalist aspirations, and to negotiate with the Indian leaders to reach some compromise. Consider the

Morley-Minto reforms of 1909 the announced purpose of which was to associate the Indians "with the government in decisions on public questions." Consider the Government of India Act of 1919 establishing a quasi-federal system in which the majority of members were to be elected. Consider the round table conferences of 1930 and 1931 in London to seek an understanding with the nationalist leaders. Consider the Government of India Act of 1935, which provided for greater provincial autonomy, and under which the franchise was extended to some 30 million persons. In fact the elections to the provincial assemblies were held in 1937, and in 5 provinces regular congress governments were installed to govern their areas. Consider the famous mission of Sir Stafford Cripps of 1942 to India when, on behalf of the British Government, he proposed that once the war was over, the British Government would work with Indian representatives for "the creation of the new Indian Union." And finally consider the efforts of Lord Wavell, the Viceroy of India, in October 1943 to form his new executive council in consultation with the Indian leaders. But all this fell short of the Indian nationalist aspirations. When the British were ready to make some concessions, the Indian nationalist movement had gone ahead demanding greater rights; and when the colonial power had finally got around to the idea of giving large autonomy at the provincial level, the Indians were no more prepared to accept anything that was short of complete independence of the nation. It was this widening gap between British intentions and Indian national aspirations that acted as a real accelerator in ramping up the mass base of Indian nationalism. And, it was finally this situation which finally made the British accede to the Indian demand of the total transfer of power in 1947. But this was not the only factor. There were others. There was the coming into power of the Labour Party, which was more favourably inclined to Indian independence. There was the considerable weakening of Great Britain as a defining power in the aftermath of World War II, and its consequent inability to effectively defend its imperial interests; and last, but not least, there were considerable international pressures—particularly emanating from the United States—on London to give India its independence. It was combination of all these factors that finally instigated the British to begin the process of negotiations in 1945 in order to transfer power to the Indians.

The Rise of Muslim Nationalism

Thus through the years, the Indian nationalist movement, under Tilak, Gokhale and Gandhi, moved from strength to strength finally becoming massive and embracing the Gandhian goal of the independence of the country. But the leadership of these great historic figures, which had given the movement a certain perception and vigour, was also the cause of its disruption. While underlining the basic cultural and religious unity of the people they invariably invoked its roots in Hinduism. Often they had declared that India had always been a nation because of its religious and cultural unity. They had revived the memories of the greatness of the Hindu kings and eulogised their heroic deeds ; and more often than not they had delved deeply into Hindu religious literature in order to stress the age-old fundamental unity of India. Even Gandhi—politically the most secular of them all—freely used

Hindu terminology that was charged with deep religious emotions, harkening back to the golden age of peace and prosperity when Rama, revered by Hindus as a God, ruled over men. "After all," he wrote, "there is something in Hinduism that has kept it alive up till now. It has witnessed the fall of Babylonian, Syrian, Persian and Egyptian civilisations? Cast a look around you. Where is Rome and Greece? Can you find anywhere the Italy of Gibbon or rather the ancient Rome, for Rome was Italy. Go to Greece. Where is the world famous Attic Civilisation? Then come to India, let one go through the vast ancient records and then look around you and you will be constrained to say 'yes I see India here ancient India is still living.' True there are dung heaps too, here and there, but there are rich treasures buried under them. And the reason why it has survived is that the end that Hinduism set before it was not development along material but spiritual lines."[38]

For the Muslims of India, the largest minority on the subcontinent, all this was a matter of concern. What about us, they argued? Where do we fit in this great and complex framework? What about our past glories? Are they not a part of Indian history? If Hinduism is important in order to stress the religious and cultural unity of the country, then is it not logical for us to argue that we the Muslims of the subcontinent constitute a separate nation with our own culture, our own traditions and our own values?

It was these types of questions and doubts that emerged among the Muslims and finally catalysed them to begin their own socio-cultural renaissance as distinct from the Hindus.

The central figures who evoked these doubts and who had successively shaped the movement were also—like the Indian nationalists—three outstanding personalities—Sir Sayyid Ahmad, Sir Mohammad Iqbal and Mohammad Ali Jinnah. One was an educationist-reformer; the second was poet- philosopher while the third was a lawyer.

Like some of his Hindu counterparts, Sir Sayyad contributed in various ways to a synthesis of Islam and western ideas, and played a significant role in the development of a separate Muslim political consciousness. In 1875 he founded a Muslim college in Aligarh (now Aligarh University) and believed that the Muslims should preserve their own culture and their own institutions, but should, at the same time play the role of a subordinate partner in the British imperial rule over India. He insistently underlined the fact that there was a Muslim consciousness quite distinct from the Hindus and for this reason discouraged the Muslims from any participation in the Indian National congress.

Sayyid's determination to hold the Muslims aloof from the mainstream of what was generally considered Indian nationalism was the first overt step to a separate political existence. A democratic regime, argued Sayyid, means a majority rule, and a majority rule in India would mean Hindu rule. Therefore, the British cannot be dispensed with, and the Muslims should concentrate on fitting themselves to take their place in the State which the numbers justified.

This position lasted until the great rising of the national feeling connected with the partition of Bengal in 1905 which presaged some extension of the Indian share in the administration by the Government. The thought of elections sounded the tocsin of alarm in Muslim minds, and there then unfolded that process under which each constitutional advance was accompanied by a Muslim demand for safeguards—safeguards that took the form of special or separate constituencies for Muslims on the ground that property qualifications would always place them in a minority on account of their poverty compared to the Hindus. In 1906 Lord Minto admitted to a deputation of notables that their claim for separate electorates, and this was followed by the formation of the Muslim League in December 1906 whose main objective was to protect the political and other rights of Indian Muslims.

When one listens to the sound of history, it cannot be denied that the whole demand and movement of Muslim separation was the authentic voice of a community deeply concerned of its fate in a united and independent India. The British policy of divide and rule, compounded with the increasing Hinduisation of the nationalist movement, may have contributed to the expansion of this ongoing process, but it was not the determining factor, for the determining factor was really the Muslims themselves who wanted to live in an independent world of their own.

If Sir Sayyid Ahmad played a crucial role in germinating Muslim consciousness in which separate electorates was finally a concrete political manifestation, it was the great poet, Mohammad Iqbal—equally fearful of losing a Muslim majority in a United India—went further. As a "poet of islamic reawakening in India in the 20th century,"[39] he gave an intellectual direction to the Muslim separatist movement and helped in the formulation of the concept of Muslim nationalism that led to the demand of a separate Muslim state. To preserve separate identities, he proposed the amalgamation of Muslims in the Northwest into a single State. "I would like to see the Punjab, Northwest Frontier Province, Sindh and Baluchistan amalgamated into a single State."[40] His ideas were reiterated in his letters to Jinnah in 1936 and 1937 with an emphasis on a separate federation of Muslim provinces to "save Muslims from the domination of non-Muslims."

But, Mohammad Ali Jinnah took a much greater leap in this ongoing process of Muslim nationalism by expounding the two-nation theory, and by demanding a separate independent Muslim State. If Sayyid and Iqbal—driven by fear of losing Muslim identity in a vast Hindu sea—were proposing benign solutions that would protect them, Jinnah took the whole idea of Muslim nationalism to its quintessential conclusion by proposing a separate State for the Muslims on the ground that they were a separate nation, and as such deserved a mastery over their own destiny. Thus on 22 March 1940 Jinnah demanded a separate homeland for the Muslims at the Lahore session of the Muslim League, which was attended by tens of thousands from all parts of India. It was the largest gathering to come together so far—undoubtedly a sign of the attractiveness of the whole idea of partition. On 23 March a resolution to that effect was moved and on 24 March it was adopted at the Lahore session. Jinnah's formula thus became the official creed of the Muslim League.[41]

But, let it be noted that Jinnah was no religious fundamentalist, nor did his lifestyle follow, even remotely, any of the Islamic codes. Essentially he was secular person. And his demand for a separate Muslim State was based on his political judgement that the future of the Muslim community would be jeopardised and threatened in a united India that would be unavoidably underpinned by a Hindu majority.

One of the crucial factors that galvanised Jinnah in the direction of the two nation theory was the elections of 1937 in UP. The Congress Party refused to form a coalition government with the Muslim League—though an understanding to this effect had been informally reached. Jawaharlal Nehru and Maulana Azad had declared to the league representatives that "the Muslim League group in the United Provinces" will have to "cease to function as a separate group" and will have to join the Congress "as full members."[42]

In effect the Congress was striving to literally dissolve the Muslim League on the ground that , in Nehru's words, it "represents a group pf Muslims...that have no contact with the Muslim masses and few even with the Muslim lower middle class."[43]

The failure of the establishment of Congress-League coalition in UP—principally due to the Congress Party's arrogance and disaffection—clearly was an important event that heavily marked Jinnah's actions in later years i.e., his refusal to have any understanding with the Congress Party.

History should judge him differently from the rigid and almost dogmatic demonisation of Jinnah that has persisted in all Indian evaluations of his life and politics.

Interestingly the new and growing reappraisal of his life and politics has emanated from political personalities belonging to the right wing of Indian politics.[44] Jaswant Singh's latest book, projecting a favourable picture of Jinnah, has divided the BJP and has resulted in his expulsion from the party.

Muslim nationalism was thus firmly locked on the road to seeking its own separate identity; and there was no hope of the re-emergence of an integrated Indian nationalism of which the Hindus and Muslims would constitute the two pillars. There were now two distinct nationalisms which evolved in two different directions with contradictory objectives. The one, the Congress Party, wanting to maintain the territorial integrity of India, whereas the other, the Muslim League, was aiming at the establishment of a separate State for the Muslims. The British may have perceived this incongruous development in a favourable light since it opened the possibilities of following the age-long maxim of divide and rule. But, when, after World War II, the two irreconcilable nationalisms became increasingly confrontational, ramping up the scale of tensions between the communities, the British were unable to manage the growing crisis. Greatly weakened by the strains of the war, they did not know how to handle the dimensional crisis that was rapidly emerging on the subcontinent. How should they handle it now that it was becoming clearly evident that the war had considerably debilitated the British making it virtually impossible for them to hold on to their imperial interests—least of all in gigantic India? To whom could they transfer power? To which political party could they assign the responsibility of running independent India?

Should they now insist upon maintaining the territorial integrity of the entire nation, when they had for decades did attempt to divide the two communities? How should they unravel the harm that had already been done? Should they just withdraw, and leave India to its fate? Was there really no risk involved in their rapid and unilateral withdrawal? Would it not plunge the whole nation into a blood bath?

This was the conundrum that they were faced with in the aftermath of World War 11, when they had—for once—seriously begun to think of pacifically transferring power in India through a heightened process of negotiations with all the parties concerned. This was indeed, historically, the greatest and the most peaceful act for the transfer of power on the subcontinent.

References

1. Cited in Nirad C. Chauduri, *The Autobiography of an Unknown Indian",* London : Picador 1999, p. 401.
2. For details, see Radha Kumud Mookerji, *The Fundamental Unity of India,* London : Chronicle Books, 2004.
3. Cited in ibid, p. 37.
4. D.S. Sharma, *Hinduism through the Ages,* Bombay : Bharatiya Bhavan, 2000, p. 4.
5. *Eastern and Western Desciples: The Life of Swami Vivekananda,* Calcutta : Advaita Ashram 1960.
6. A.R. Desai, *Social Background of Indian Nationalism,* Bombay: Popular Prakashan, 1966, p. 292.
7. Cited in Jawaharlal Nehru, *Discovery of India,* Calcutta: The Signet Press, 1946, p. 339.
8. Cited in K.C.Vyas, *The Social Renaissance of India,* Bombay: Vohra & Co. 1957, p. 105.

9. Cited in M.A. Buch, *Rise and Growth of Indian Militant Nationalism,* Baroda : Atmaram Press, 1940, p. 174.
10. For this model of nationalism see Geoffrey Barraclough, *An Introduction to Contemporary History,* Harmondsworth : Penguin Books, 1967.
11. Philip Mason, *The Men who Ruled India*, London: Pan Books, 1985, p. 178.
12. Penderel Moon, *The British Conquest and Dominion of India,* London: Duckworth, 1989, p. 652.
13. J.R. Seeley, *Expansion of England,* London: Macmillan, 1886, p. 35.
14. R.C.Majumdar (General Editor), *British Paramountcy and Indian Renaissance Part 1* Bombay: Bharatiya Vidya Bhavan, 1963, p. 469.
15. Sir Percival Griffth, *The British Impact on India,* London: Cass, 1965.
16. Surendra Nath Sen, *Eighteen Fifty Seven* , New Delhi: Publications Division, 1957, p. 297.
17. S.B. Chaudhri, *Civil Rebellion in the Indian mutinies,* Calcutta: World Press, 1957, p. 200.
18. Sir Percival Spear, *The British Impact on India,* Cambridge: Archos Books, 1965, p. 279.
19. M.C. Buch, *Rise and Growth of Militant Indian Nationalism,* op. cit., p. 151.
20. Sir William Wedderburn, *Allan Octavian Hume,* New Delhi : Commonwealth Publishers, 1989, p. 101.
21. Ibid. p. 47.
22. Rupert Emerson, *From Empire to a Nation. The Rise to Self-Assertion of Asian and African Peoples,* Boston: Beacon Press, 1960, p. 10.
23. *Congress Presidential Addresses: The Indian National Congress,* Madras: 1917, p. 4.
24. Ibid.
25. Ibid., p. 91.
26. Cited in D.C. Gupta, *Indian National Movement,* Delhi: Vikas Publications, 1970, p. 37.

27. Patabhi Sitaramayya, *The History of the Indian National Congress 2nd edition,* Vol. 1 Bombay: Padma Publications, 1946, p. 89.
28. Sir Percival Spear, *India,* London: Oxford University Press, 1949, p. 315.
29. Sir Valantine Choril, *Indian Unrest,* London: Elibron Series, 1926, p. 115.
30. Cited in Annie Besant, *India: A Nation,* Madras: Format Book, 1923, p. 128.
31. Cited in R.C. Majumdar (edited), *Struggle for Freedom,* Bombay: Bhartiya Vidya Bhavan, 1969, p. 77.
32. *Modern Review,* No. 1 1945, p. 287.
33. For details about Tilak, see Dhananjay Keer, *Lokamanya Tilak,* Bombay: Popular Prakashan, 1969.
34. Cited in M.A, Buch, op. cit., pp. 145-146
35. Jahawarlal Nehru, op. cit, p. 361.
36. Ibid, p. 365.
37. Valji Govindji Desai (translated and edited), *The Diary of Mahadev Desai,* Vol. 1, Ahmedabad: Navjivan Publishing House, 1953, p.12.
38. M.K. Gandhi, *Hindu Dharma,* Ahmedabad: Navjivan Publishing House,1950, p. 54.
39. Mohammad Ali, *My Life:A Fragment,* Lahore: SH Mohammad Ashraf, 1966, p. 177.
40. Cited in Rafiq Zakaria, *The Widening Divide: An Insight into Hindu-Muslim Relations,* New Delhi: Viking, 1995, p. 51.
41. For details about Jinnah, see Sikandar Hayat, *The Charismatic Leader: Quaid-i-Azam Mohammad Ali Jinnah and the Creation of Pakistan,* Oxford: Oxford University Press, 2008.
42. For details, see A.G. Noorani's book review article "Partition retrospect," in *Frontline,* 25 September 2009, p. 82.
43. Ibid., p. 80.
44. Jaswant Singh, *Jinnah India-Partition Independence*, New Delhi: Rupa, 2009.

3

Independence

This bill is a moral to all future generations. It is a treaty of peace without a war

Lord Samuel 1947

The process of transferring power really began during World War II. The British Government had realised that it could no longer hold on to India; for pressures were indeed ratcheting up that it could no longer resist—pressures from the Indian nationalists who were insisting on the British departure and who were threatening to launch a massive nationalist revolt; from the US Administration which favoured Indian independence, including President Roosevelt personally through letters to and personal interaction with Churchill; from the invasive Japanese who were knocking at the doors of India and threatening the very future of the British empire; from the anti-British activities of Subhas Chandra Bose, who, according to

Clement Atlee, was weakening "the very foundation of the attachment of the Indian land and naval forces to the British Government;"[1] and from Clement Atlee (Labour Party) who warned Churchill that his views were "not widely shared" and his imperialist policies were "fatally short-sighted and suicidal"[2] Equally important was the writer Patrick French's argumentation that the British had "lost control over crucial areas of the administration and lacked the will and the financial or military ability to recover that control."[3]

The first serious British attempt to transfer power was made in 1942 during the height of World War II. Stafford Cripps, a labour party icon and Lord Privy Seal in Churchill's War Cabinet, known for his sympathy for India and his friendship for Nehru, was mandated in March-April 1942 to offer Indians a Constituent Assembly, within a year after the termination of hostilities, that would have the sovereign authority to decide the future of India. Under the scheme India could opt to remain within the Commonwealth or become completely independent.[4]

Cripps encountered all sorts of obstacles. His proposals never really got off the ground. They faced obstructive opposition from the British themselves, Linlithgow, the Viceroy who hardly favoured independence, and particularly denounced Cripps' underlying idea to abridge his veto powers to overrule the proposed interim government; Leo Amery, the Secretary of India, who favoured the holding on to India as long as possible and demanded the incorporation of the so-called "provincial option" that would have left the door open to separatism; and, of course, there was Prime Minister Churchill, arch-opponent of any liquidation of the Empire, who did everything to render Cripps' mission a failure. Whenever Cripps reached a crucial stage in his negotiations, the trio went into action to constrain him.[5]

The Congress Party also gave short shrift to Cripps. For the essentials of the proposal pertaining to the Constituent Assembly were to become operational only in the future once the war was over. Mahatma Gandhi compared them to a post-dated cheque "on a bank that is obviously failing."[6] Indeed there was deep-seated scepticism among Congress leaders that Britain may not honour the obligation. Besides there was the famous "opting out" clause which would have allowed any Indian province to cede out of the new Independent State—a stipulation that the Congress leaders perceived as "an important concession to Muslim separatism,[7] thus opening the constitutional path for the creation of Pakistan.

The Congress countered the proposal with its own demand for an immediate handing over of power, and decided to launch the "Quit India" movement in August 1942. Apparently the party had arrived at the conclusion that, with the British on the defensive, now was the time to strike. But, it was a wrongly calculated move, for the British, in no mood to yield to such drastic demands in the midst of a difficult global conflict, struck back promptly by arresting the entire Congress leadership, by declaring the organisation illegal. and by banning all demonstrations of more than 5 persons. With most of the leaders behind bars, the Quit India movement did'nt take off in an significant way. It had no real massive impact on the country, and did not generate much turbulence—at least not enough to shake the British determination to continue with the status quo. If anything, the Congress Party came out of this confrontational trial as a loser. The behaviour of political actors had become obdurate; and the configuration of forces had skewed. The political negotiations with the British, centred around Cripps proposal, were frozen—negotiations which could have finally taken India to an orderly independence. Even if the British "option clause" had been invoked by some, the risk of the partition of the subcontinent on broad Hindu-Muslim lines could have been avoided. In 1942, the Muslim League did not have a sold mass base among the Muslims. There were myriad Muslim leaders in the Muslim majority provinces who were not willing to go along with Jinnah's demand for Pakistan. Consider the North Western Frontier Province and Baluchistan; the Muslim league hardly had any real roots to speak of. If anything, it was the Congress Party which had a solid hold in the two provinces. Consider, even the crucial States of Punjab and Sind. Many Muslim provincial leaders, having a hold on the two provinces, particularly Sikandar Hayat Khan, did not belong to the Muslim League, and were not any great proponents of Pakistan. They had their own politics and their own political ambitions.

From the hindsight of more than 60 years, and the archival documentation that has surfaced it would seem that the risks of a break-up of India were minimal at the time since much of Muslim League's base was essentially in the Hindu majority areas. Pakistan seemingly could have been avoided.

But things began to change after 1942. While the Congress leaders were languishing in prison, Jinnah, with the active support of Wavell and Linlithgow, seized the opportunity to expand his influence among the Muslims. He countered Congress' "Quit India" movement by pledging a "complete loyalty" to the British of the Muslim troops, and through the electoral process that was operational at the time, managed to capture provincial Legislative seats which would later form Pakistan. It paved the way for Jinnah to strengthen the Muslim League's claims for the creation of the Pakistan State, so much so that when the next negotiatory process began, "the Muslim League had made so much progress among India's Islamic community that it could claim equal standing with the Congress."[8] This was indeed a landmark development and a turning point in contemporary Indian history; for the Congress was really no more the only major actor on the political landscape.

But there was another major ramification of British-Muslim League cooperation: the majority of British civil servants in India, who were known to be traditionally pro-Muslim,[9] now became sympathetic to the idea of creating Pakistan. Even the Viceroy, Wavell, hitherto known to be non-committal in his attitude to the two communities, gave unabashed support for Jinnah and the Muslim League. Arguably he began to show signs of supporting the idea that the establishment of Pakistan would be geo-politically in British interest since it should then be possible to contain any Soviet expansion in the oil—rich gulf area. In a secret telegram of 6th February 1946 he "commended" to the Secretary of India the partition of the subcontinent.[10] Though Wavell had certainly evoked the idea, no new evidence has surfaced to suggest that the British Government had officially rallied to this recommendation in early 1946.

Winston Churchill, on the other hand, was one of the leading conservatives who was a consistent proponent of the partition of India. While, there is no hard evidence to suggest that there was any secret understanding between Jinnah and Churchill for the formation of Pakistan, extensive correspondence between them does show Churchill's keen interest in the Muslim League. In a letter to Jinnah he did declare that any Muslim State that may be established should remain in the Commonwealth.[11]

The second phase in the ongoing negotiatory process was Wavell's convocation of a conference in July 1945—a conference of all political parties—the underlying purpose of which was to expand the Viceroy's Executive Council during the war's duration. Jinnah was the real star at the conference, since none of the Congress national leaders were invited as they did not fall within the categories for participation designated by Wavell.

While it was perceived as a gigantic "charade from beginning to end" by an Indian observer[12], it did have a beneficial effect on Jinnah since it gave him the opportunity to make Pakistan as the central issue. The Muslim leader made it clear that no interim arrangement, proposed at the conference, would be acceptable as long as the proposal for the establishment of Pakistan was not accepted. He feared that "the future Executive will work as a unitary government of India" that will settle down "for an unlimited period" and thus jeopardise all his plans for establishing Pakistan.[13] The Conference thus failed.

Labour Party Initiative

The next negotiatory process was inaugurated after the electoral victory of the Labour Party in July 1945 arousing great expectations, and raising urgent questions regarding India's future political status.

Now that the political situation had changed in England many on the subcontinent wondered how the new government was going to respond to India's persistent demand for independence, and how the new Labour Party leaders—favourably disposed to Indian independence—were going to handle the intractable problem of dual and conflicting nationalisms of the two principal communities of India.

To the relief and satisfaction of most Indians the basic British response was positive. The Viceroy of India, Wavell,[14] who had gone to London to seek instructions from the new government announced on his return in mid-September 1945, "His Majesty's Government determination to do its utmost to promote, in conjunction with the Indian opinion, the early realisation of the full self-government in India".[15] Also he announced that elections to the Central and Provincial Legislatures—so long postponed owing to the war—would be held "during the coming cold weather," and that soon after the publications of the election results, steps would be taken "to bring into being an Executive Council which will have the support of the main Indian parties."[16]

The elections were held in late 1945. They confirmed the politico-religious division of the country. While the Congress remained the strongest party among the Hindus, the Muslim League, continuing to expand since 1942, had now acquired an equal hold over the Muslim population. The two-nations theory—until then an abstract notion—now clearly found a palpable political expression. Also, it became quite evident by 1945 that while the Congress had the capacity of blocking any solution offered by the British that was short of independence, the Muslim League could now equally impede any plan that did not meet its demand of partition of the subcontinent.

In addition to these omens of discord there were also palpable portents that British power was undergoing a radical change during these historic moments. That is to say that the British ability to impose decisions or even to maintain the status quo was rapidly dwindling. The old attitude of "we will hold the ring until the two parties come to an agreement" was no longer possible because neither the clout nor the moral conviction were there to sustain it. Besides, the British elections had made it amply clear that the public was in no mood to make any sacrifices to maintain British supremacy in India. Furthermore, power was now in the hands of new decision makers who were proponents of Indian independence, and who were, therefore, prepared to recognise the emerging realities of the new situation. The only question that remained was how soon can power be handed over and in what manner. An additional effect of this new mood in Britain was the rapid demobilisation of the armed forces—a demobilisation that resulted in the disappearance of most military units by the Spring of 1946. No longer it had much physical force at its disposal to impose its way or to quell any disorder. The only alternative now left was to peacefully negotiate solutions before leaving the subcontinent.

The Cabinet Mission

It was in this mood that the Labour Government made its major move to accelerate Indian independence. In the Spring of 1946 a special high powered mission, composed of three members of the Cabinet—Lord Pethwick Lawrence, Secretary of State for India, Sir Stafford Cripps, President of the Board of trade, and A.V. Alexander, First Lord of the Admiralty—arrived in India with the intention of making the supreme effort to break the deadlock between Britain and the Indians on the one hand, and the Congress Party and the Muslim League on the other.

The aim of the mission was to persuade the Indian leaders to formulate their own scheme for independence, for this, it was felt, was the only viable manner in which power could be effectively transferred. But, it did not take them very long to realise that the traditional stand-off between the Congress and the Muslim League had created such ill-feeling and such animosity that it seemed impossible to get them to agree even on the very fundamentals of national unity. Jinnah, the leader of the Muslim League, had created a very difficult climate for smooth negotiations by his cold, arrogant and insistent demand for Pakistan or nothing. Displaying great confidence and determination in reaching his objective, he would appear, in the sweltering heat of Delhi, before the Cabinet Mission in immaculately cut Western clothes—never relaxing no matter what friendly overture they made to him. When one looks at the history of the period, it is indeed undeniable that Jinnah was very firm in his objectives—a firmness that many criticised as gigantically unreasonable, but which was nonetheless a sign of his steadfast leadership in the face of all the pressures he was facing from the British as well as the Congress Party.

Maulana Abul Kalam Azad, the Congress President, and one of the party's representatives at the negotiations, on the other hand, was a very different person. In fact. he was just the opposite of Jinnah. He emblematised India. As a devout Muslim, he garbed himself in traditional Indian fashion, had no exposure to modern western education, had no apparent knowledge of the English language, and had none of the arrogant accoutrements that surrounded Jinnah's personality. The Cabinet mission, it would seem "gained their greatest comfort" from him.[17] To counter Jinnah, Azad, made a powerful case against the partition of the country. He naturally sympathised with the legitimate fears of India's 90 million Muslims of the dangers of being swamped by the powerful Hindu majority—fears he stressed needed to be addressed seriously. But, he always refused to believe Jinnah's plan of Pakistan was a viable and credible solution. He argued that the very idea of Pakistan was a symbol of defeatism, and an acknowledgement of the unacceptable reasoning that Muslims could not establish their identity in a multi-religious and multi-cultural environment. It was wrong, he insisted, to draw an analogy with the Jewish demand for a national homeland, because the Muslims already had one in India. The creation of Pakistan, therefore, would not only fail to give any benefits to the Muslims but in fact would be detrimental to their interests. If two States were created,—Pakistan out of Muslim majority provinces and India out of the Hindu majority provinces—then what about 25 per cent Muslims scattered in small minorities all over India? Who is going to defend them? Would the 17 per cent Muslims in the United Provinces, 12 per cent in Bihar and 9 per cent in Madras not become weaker and even more insecure than ever before in the Hindu majority provinces. He was convinced that "the demand for Pakistan loses all force. As a Muslim, I for one am not prepared for a moment to give up my right to treat the whole of India as my domain, and to share in the shaping of its political and economic life. To me it seems a sure sign of cowardice to give up what is my patrimony and content myself with a mere fragment of it."[18]

Azad proposed instead a formula under which full autonomy would be accorded to the Indian provinces with the Central Government responsible for Defence, Foreign Affairs, and Communications. Such a proposal, he argued, "ensures the Muslim majority provinces are internally free to develop as they will, but can at the same time influence the Centre on all issues which effect India as a whole."[19]

Here was an interesting, and, in many ways, an original proposal by a man who was concerned and preoccupied with the future of Muslims, and who was determined to find a solution to this seemingly intractable problem within the Indian framework. But the Muslim League leaders were not prepared to accept it. Was it because these were the proposals that emanated from a Muslim who was a persona non grata with the Muslim League? Was it because they had the backing of the Congress Party in whom they had no confidence? Or was it because it fell short of some stipulation that would have allowed the provinces to secede should they decide to do so? Whatever may have been the reasons, one thing was clear: there was a total impasse between the political parties, and it seemed that the Cabinet Mission may well be jeopardised.

When this became evident that the parties were unable or unwilling to reach an agreement on their own, the Mission decided to opt for the second alternative: to themselves work out a plan. Basically the British scheme followed Azad's idea that the Central Government would be responsible for only three subjects: foreign affairs, defence and communications. The unity of India would be maintained. For the rest the country would be divided into three main administrative groups. Group A would comprise most of India where Hindus were in a majority. Group B would be composed of Punjab. Sind, the North Western Frontier Province and Baluchistan where Muslims had a large majority, while Group C would consist of Bengal and Assam where the Muslims had a small majority. Thus the Muslim minority would be responsible for their own domestic affairs and would be protected from any danger of Hindu domination. A Constituent Assembly would be created to draw up a constitution for the new Union. In the meantime an interim government, composed of representatives of major political parties, would administer the country pending the complete transfer of power. Though the basic idea of enlarged autonomy was the one proposed by Azad, there were nonetheless four major British additions. One was that the provinces were grouped together in three large administrative zones. Though broadly based on religious lines each of them would be large enough to govern themselves efficaciously. The second was an interim government through which the major parties would provisionally administer India The third was that a Constituent Assembly, composed of the whole of India, would draw a constitution for a united India. And the fourth was that while the provinces could not secede from the group during the time that the Constitution was being drafted, the group itself as a whole, after a time frame, could withdraw from the Union. It was indeed an ingenuous proposal, which, while giving a try to the unity of India, contained the possibility of opting for secession should it be desired, and should it become unavoidable.

To the surprise of everyone, both sides accepted the proposals. Both of them had certain reservations, but the executive committees of the two organisations, after long deliberations, signified their willingness to work with the plan.

Peace at last appeared to be at hand. Independence appeared to be round the corner. For the first time in the history of negotiations for the transfer of power the two political parties appeared to be on the same wave length.

But this joy was alas premature, for within weeks escalating difference of interpretations of the agreement surfaced. And the negotiations were back to square one.

What happened? What went wrong? How come that the happy results of long and painful negotiations did not last long? Was any body really responsible for this state of affairs, or was it the result of the serious suspicion that prevailed on both sides?

It is true that Jinnah was always suspicious of Congress' motives and intentions. He really did not trust its party leaders. To some extent this was based on past experience. The Muslim League, often in the past, had concluded political agreements with Congress, and had fought elections on a joint platform with the clear stipulation that when the elections were won the Muslim League would have its share of place in the provincial governments. But, wherever Congress secured a majority of seats—as was the case in 1935 in United Provinces—and no longer needed Muslim League help, it repudiated the agreements and offered the League a single unimportant portfolio—or none at all. Jinnah feared the repeat of a similar situation. But this was not the only reason, though this is already significant and weighty. There existed, among the Muslim League leaders, that psychological and irrational distrust of the Hindus which is rather difficult to define. It pervaded the political atmosphere but it alluded you when you tried to grasp it, define it and to understand it. It was always there in the background as a permanent landscape the heavy burden of which India has carried it throughout its modern history. Jinnah had, therefore, accepted the Cabinet mission proposal for a united India only because there was a stipulation in the agreement that the Administrative groups could secede from the Union should they decide to do so. It is indeed unlikely that he would have accepted any proposal that did not give him such a possibility. As long as such a possibility existed that could eventually be invoked, Jinnah presumably did not wish to be projected as a person who always said no to any proposal that were made by the British for the transfer of power. It is, therefore, incorrect to suggest that Jinnah had abandoned his goal of Pakistan by accepting the Cabinet mission proposal. He had not. He never had. There is considerable evidence available to this effect, the most recent of which is Hamayun Mirza's recent biography of his father Iskander Mirza who was Pakistan's first President in 1958.[20] Based upon his father's testimony to him, Hamayun Mirza records that in February 1947 Jinnah declared to Iskander Mirza, who was a senior civil servant in the Indian government at the time, "that if Pakistan could not be won by negotiations, it would have to be won by the will of the Muslims." According to this testimony, Jinnah "asked Iskander Mirza to be prepared to resign from the Government of India, and return to the tribal territory that he knew so well. There he was to start a jihad (holy war) against the British."[21] Commenting on Jinnah in his book, Hamayun Mirza unequivocally declares that the Muslim League leader was "prepared to go to any length to achieve Pakistan.... Once he made up his mind, he would pursue a single objective with tenacious zeal."[22]

Therefore when Jawaharlal Nehru, on becoming the President of the Congress, began to give his own personal interpretations to the Cabinet Mission proposal, that was virtual re-negotiations of the agreement reached by the two parties Jinnah seized the opportunity to denounce the agreement.

Apparently Nehru was not happy with the agreement. As a member of the Congress High Command he had accepted the Cabinet Mission Plan, but his subsequent actions seem to indicate that he had done so primarily because he felt that he would be outvoted should he oppose it. Now that he had become Congress President he showed his reservations regarding the plan, and his undisguised contempt of the Muslim League and its leader Jinnah. On 10 July 1946 he called a press conference to discuss his policy as the head of the party. It was a delicate moment in India's history, and what was needed was circumspection, restraint and diplomacy to avoid any declaration that would rock the boat. Instead Nehru chose this very moment to launch into what his biographer, Michael Brecher, has termed as "one of the most fiery and provocative statements in his forty years of his public life."[23] Indeed it was fiery. And, indeed it was provocative. For, when he was asked by Press representatives whether his Party's approval of the Plan meant that he had accepted it in toto, Nehru replied with some petulance that the Congress was "completely unfettered by agreement and free to meet all situations as they arise." He made it clear that the Congress was committed to participate in the Constituent Assembly; and the Assembly would be a sovereign body, regardless of statements from London. Of course, he said, the protection of the minorities had to be assured, as the Congress had always pledged, but this would be done by the Constituent Assembly. Regarding the grouping scheme he was even more brutally candid. It would, probably, never come to fruition, he declared, since group A, the Hindu majority provinces would be opposed, the NWFP would oppose it in group B as would Assam in group C. He also stressed the likelihood of a much stronger central government than envisaged by the Cabinet Mission. "The scope of the Centre," he declared "even though limited inevitably grows because it cannot exist otherwise."[24]

Admittedly there was much political insight in what Nehru said, for it was simply not possible to link India's future to a loosely worded unchangeable plan. But, the fact is that the plan was there, accepted by both the parties. By making such frank observations, he destroyed the very façade of the agreement. Undoubtedly this was a big mistake. For one does not begin to question an agreement that had been consensually agreed upon by all the parties concerned.

It would be of course incorrect to suggest that it was only Nehru who undermined the delicately packaged compromise that the British had advanced, and which was to remain untouched even by the Constituent Assembly, and which had to be accepted by members of the Constituent Assembly as a precondition to their nomination to the assembly. The British wanted this to be sine quo non. For it was Gandhi too who rocked the boat by enunciating the idea that the proposal could be interpreted unilaterally by the provinces. "The provinces," he wrote in his journal. *Harijan* on 17 May 1946 "were free to reject the very idea of grouping. No province could be forced against its will to belong to a group even if the idea of grouping was accepted."[25] In fact, Gandhi had made it clear to the Mission on 24 June that they were "law givers and could not interpret their own law."[26]

Paradoxically the two leaders (Gandhi and Nehru), who were determined to maintain the unity of the country, were the ones who undermined it by making outlandish statements that brought to an end all the British Mission's efforts to keep the country united. They and their party, according to Cripps' biographer, "hedged about with potentially disabling reservations, notably over grouping of provinces."[27]

Jinnah reacted immediately. To him all this was a confirmation of his fears that the Hindu majority could not be trusted. Jinnah declared that Nehru had in effect completely repudiated the Cabinet Mission Plan. Now that the new Congress President had declared that his party could change the scheme through its majority in the Constituent Assembly this would mean that the minority would be at the mercy of the majority. The Muslim League Council met in Bombay on 27th July and withdrew its acceptance of the Cabinet Mission Plan. In his opening speech, Jinnah reiterated the demand for Pakistan as the only course now open to the Muslim League. The Council then passed a resolution authorising the Working Committee to draw a plan of "Direct Action"[28], and called upon all members of the League to renounce any titles they may have received from the British Government. The Muslim League leader commented "what we have done today is the most historic act in our history. Never have we in the whole history of the League done anything except by constitutional methods and by constitutionalism. But now we are obliged and forced into this position. This day we bid good-bye to constitutional methods."[29] He recalled that throughout the fateful negotiations with the Cabinet Mission both the British and the Congress had held a pistol in their hands, the one of authority and arms, and the other of mass-struggle and non-cooperation. "Today," he declared, "we have also forged a pistol and are in a position to stake it."[30] Jinnah, the lawyer, was now projecting himself in a new garb—the garb of a mass leader.

It remains unclear why Jinnah had accepted the principle of the unity of India. Was it that he was under considerable pressure, and had calculated that Pakistan would materialise anyway—if not today then tomorrow—since the Muslim majority groups could always withdraw from the Indian Union. In any event one thing is certain: Jinnah had never abandoned his goal of establishing Pakistan. To suggest that he had—as some do—goes against all indications of the period."[31]

It is important to note that while the British Labour Government and the public opinion generally favoured the idea of leaving India united, there were important British personalities who favoured the partition of the country There was Beverley Nichols who had openly argued in his book, *Verdict on India,* that Britain could not leave India without creating a separate homeland for the Muslims. But the most important, as we have seen earlier, was Winston Churchill whose vocal support to Pakistan, according to one observer, "was instrumental in creating the world's first Islamic state, and in sabotaging any last hopes of Indian unity."[32]

In any event the consequences of Nehru's action and Jinnah's reaction were horrendous. All the negotiations, so painfully carried out and so prudently agreed upon, reviving the hope of maintaining the unity of India, were now dashed to the ground. India was back to squarc one.

Realising the seriousness of the situation, the Congress Working Committee met soon after the deadlock in order to explore different possibilities of saving the rapidly tense and degenerating situation.

Azad, the real architect of the agreement, pointed out that if the situation had to be saved, the Working Committee must make it clear that the view of the Congress was expressed by the resolution passed by the All-India Congress Committee accepting the Cabinet Mission proposal in toto, and that no individual, not even the Congress President, could change it. But, the Working Committee was in a dilemmic situation. While, on the one hand, Nehru's prestige was at stake, the settlement, on the other hand, so painfully achieved, was in danger. To repudiate Nehru would be injudicious, but to abandon the Cabinet Mission Plan would ruin all chances of maintaining the unity of India.

Finally, the committee passed a resolution which made no reference to Nehru's press conference, but clearly reaffirmed the All-India Congress Committee's original decision of accepting the British Plan in its entirety. Though Cripps' biographer argues that the "Congress acceptance of the constitutional scheme(the statement of 16 May) had been hedged about with potentially disturbing reservations over grouping of provinces," the trio of the Cripps were no better since "they had refrained from escaping the ambiguity" on the ground that this was a practical problem "to be resolved by the increasing momentum of actual transfer of power."[33] The Muslim League was urged to return to its earlier position. But it was too late. Jinnah refused, and held that Nehru's position represented the real mind of the Congress.

He argued that if the congress could change so many times while the British were still in the country, what assurances could the minorities have once they have left. Indeed a valid reflection.

Interim Government

However, notwithstanding this serious pressure of events—including an urgent need to establish a representative interim government—did not leave any choice on the Viceroy but to go ahead with the Cabinet Mission's plan of transferring power.

Since the Congress Party had made a categorical statement accepting the plan, The Viceroy requested Jawaharlal Nehru to form the government. Nehru accepted the proposal. However, before taking any steps in this direction, and presumably realising that it was his famous statement of 10 July that had generated a deadlock, he decided to approach Jinnah.

It was an hard decision, since Nehru had a low opinion of Jinnah and considered him insincere, opportunist and a snob who had left the Congress Party in the early years "only because it ceased to be a party for gentleman."[34] Therefore to have to ask favours of Jinnah whose stubbornness was legendary, and, at the same time, to have to admit to himself that it was his own maladroitness that was really responsible for the deadlocked situation must have been even harder; but he did swallow his pride and drove to Jinnah's sumptuous house on Malabar Hill in Bombay to persuade him to join him in the formation of an interim government.

The response was absolutely negative. Jinnah was polite but unyielding. The interview was not only abortive, but after it was over the antipathy between the two men was greater than ever before. For Jinnah, the "arrogant Brahmin" could not be relied upon and for Nehru the "fascist demagogue" was standing in the way of India's freedom.

As Nehru drove away from Malabar Hill he could clearly see the black flags of mourning—the banners proclaiming "Direct Action Day" flying from Muslim houses and outside of the shuttered Muslim shops. But Bombay was a Hindu majority area and there was no trouble. Sind and the Punjab, two of the majority Muslim areas of India, were also under control since Muslims there were still fearful of the idea of Pakistan. They were still not convinced that it was really in their interest.

However away on the eastern side of India in the big city of Calcutta, Muslim League's direct action had broken into bloody madness. Bengal had a Muslim majority, and in Calcutta the provincial Muslim League government, headed by H.S. Surawardy, belonged to a category of people "who believed that no politician need ever be out of office once his strong-arm squads have gained control of the polling booths, that no minister should suffer financially by being in public life that no relative or political cohort should ever go unrewarded."[35] In the beginning of August he announced that 16th of that month—the day of direct action— would be a public holiday, and when Hindus of the provincial legislative assembly protested against it, he ordered the party machine to vote for it. On 5th August he went even further. Under the *nom de plume* "Shaheed" he wrote an incendiary article in the *Statesman* of Calcutta in which he declared that "bloodshed and disorder are not necessarily evil in themselves if resorted for a noble cause. Among the Muslims, no cause is dearer or nobler than Pakistan"[36]

With all these escalatory incitements bloodshed was inevitable. In the beginning all this was left to Surawardy's professionals, but soon the scrawny downtrodden slum dwellers who followed them jumped into the fray. First of all, Hindu men, women and children were waylaid, tormented and then killed. Hindus and Sikhs retaliated. There were no pitched battles, only brutal and sudden killing of the unarmed. For four long days Calcutta became a stamping ground for the underworld which had taken over the city.

From the safety of a boat on the Hoogly River Radclyffe Sidebottom witnessed the massive killing on the river where bodies "laid on their faces with their heads poking out over Howrah bridge" were beheaded into the river, their bodies thrown in afterwards. The river, remembers Sidebottom, "was literally choked with dead bodies which floated for a while, sank for a while and, when the internal gasses blew them up, floated again after three days."[37] Another witness, Ian Stephens, was numbed almost to callousness by the "putrefying corpses stacked to the ceiling" in the morgues.[38] Official figures gave 4.000 dead and 10.000 injured. But this was a very conservative estimate, for the total casualties in these terrible four days were greater than all the communal riots that had taken place throughout the whole history of British India. Jyoti Basu, in his recent autobiography, has suggested that "by contemporary estimates the causality in the Calcutta killings in 1946 were nothing less than 20.000 or more."[39]

The moral of this terrible tragedy was that Hindus and Muslims could not live together, and that the choice for the nation was unfortunately either a civil war or a separate Muslim state. With a spill-over of Hindu-Muslim riots to the rest of India—where mutual killings were even more massive, more uncontrollable, more ubiquitous and even more brutal—the undercurrent of partition—even among its opponents— slowly began to coalesce itself.

However, despite these events, Wavell still held on to his offer to Nehru to form an interim government in accordance with the Cabinet Mission Plan. Nehru proposed to include in his team 6 Congress nominees, 3 minority representatives and 5 non-league Muslims. The Viceroy believed that it would be more judicious at this stage to leave the Muslim seats open for the time being. Nehru demurred on the ground that it will give the government the appearance of instability, and went ahead to form a government without the Muslim League.

The next step was calling a Constituent Assembly, but the stumbling block was the Congress interpretation of the grouping of provinces. While it had declared that it accepted the Cabinet Mission proposal completely, it nonetheless gave the impression of demurring on accepting unquestionably the integral unity of the three groupings—groupings on which the plan really reposed. Wavell, therefore demanded that the Congress make a categorical statement that it accepted the position that the provinces must remain in their sections as intended by the Cabinet mission, until after the first elections under the new Constitution. He also demanded assurances that the Congress will not insist on its suggestion that communal issues arriving in the Constituent Assembly be referred to the Federal Court on the ground that the communal issues were not legal in character. He warned the Congress that if it did not accept these two points, it would be difficult to convene a Constituent Assembly. The Congress Party promptly retorted that it was the moral duty of the Viceroy to call a Constituent Assembly once the interim Government was formed.

For the Viceroy the issue of calling the Assembly was a practical question not a legal one. He argued that even if the issues were referred to the Federal Court, and its ruling favoured the Congress, the party would gain nothing since the Muslim League would inevitably refuse to participate, thus delaying the whole process of constitution making when urgency was required to stem the rising communal stresses in the country. Wavell was convinced that no purpose would be served to call the Constituent Assembly as long as there was no firm agreement in advance that the groupings will not be challenged before the first elections were held under the new Constitution.

The differences were indeed very wide between the Viceroy and the Congress leaders. While Wavell did not want anything untoward to happen that would undermine the very essence of the Cabinet Mission Plan, the Congress, on the other hand, refused Wavell's interpretation of the plan, and insisted on the sovereign right of the Assembly to do what it wanted.

Negotiations were reopened to bring the Muslim League into the Interim Government. Once again the League attempted to make its conditions prevail, particularly regarding the sole right of nominating Muslims to the cabinet—a right the Congress had always refused on the ground that it was a secular organisation and could therefore nominate a Muslim to one of its seats. At last Jinnah relented on 13 October 1946. Replying to Wavell's letter he declared that as "it will be fatal to leave the entire administration of the Central government in the hands of the Congress Party" he has, he declared, " decided to nominate five members of the interim government on behalf of the Muslim League."[40] The Leagues nominees included only one of the party's leading figure, Liaquat Ali Khan, but to everyone's surprise, one of the others was not a Muslim but a member of the untouchable caste, B.R. Ambedkar who had vigorously denied Congress's right to speak for the untouchables.

Chaos in Governance

However, hardly had the agreement been reached on the new Interim Government that difficulties began to surge on an array of issues. Lacking any confidence in the Congress Party the Muslim League began to raise difficulties on all major issues.

The first major deadlocked issue was the division of portfolios among the ministers. The Viceroy believed that one of the three important portfolios –Defence, External Affairs and Home—should be given to the Muslim League. But the Congress Party was not prepared to hand over any of these portfolios. The Home Ministry was considered too important by the party strong-man, Patel, to be handed over to the League; Nehru was personally too interested in External Affairs to part with it; and the defence portfolio was in the hands of another minority community— the Sikhs— and it was not considered expedient to take it away from them.

It was, therefore. decided that the Finance Ministry would be handed over to the Muslim League Representative. The Congress leaders had wrongly calculated that since the field was too technical the League would refuse it or in any case would be unable to handle it. Jinnah promptly accepted the proposal and Liaquat Ali Khan became the Minister of Finance. Soon the Congress realised that it had made a monumental blunder in handing over finance to the Muslim league. For, in all countries the Minister in-charge of finance plays a key role in the Government, and in the new interim government set up at the time, this was even more true. With finances under his control, Liaquat Ali Khan was in a position to interfere in all other departments and held almost a veto over their policies. This crucial power became evident over the budget proposal. By imposing a 25 per cent tax on business profits over £7.500 it seriously effected the Hindu businessmen who were supporters of the Congress Party.

The second major area of conflict was the whole idea of collective responsibility of the Interim Government's Cabinet. Liaquat refused to accept Nehru's leadership for he declared that the Government was composed of two separate blocs—one Congress and the other Muslim League—each functioning under separate leaderships. As Jinnah declared "The interim Government cannot be called a Cabinet. You cannot turn a donkey into an elephant by calling it an elephant."

Third, the Muslim League decided to boycott the Constituent Assembly on the ground that the Congress Party had substantially changed the nature of the Assembly that was originally conceived by the Cabinet Mission Plan. The day the Viceroy announced that the Assembly would meet on 9th December 1946 Jinnah issued a statement declaring that this was "one more blunder of a grave and serious character" and the Viceroy was "playing in the hands of the Congress." "I want to make it clear," he went on "that no representative of the Muslim League should attend the Constituent Assembly summoned to meet on the 9th of December 1946."[41]

This new and rather unexpected development had generated another deadlock. The British Government tried to resolve it by inviting the political leaders to London for discussion. But this was of no use; for the attitudes of the two main communities became even more hardened.

And, in the meantime the great Calcutta killings spread out to other parts of India—killings that were bloodier, more brutal and more massive. There was nothing the Government could do to really contain it. Apparently the authorities had lost all control. An orderly transfer of power to a united India no longer appeared possible.

Clearly, all this was doing Jinnah's work of creating Pakistan. He could now say "even the Hindus need Pakistan—if only to save their own people from this continual slaughter and destruction. The Congress was now becoming divided on the whole question. There were those who were beginning to agree with Jinnah, but this did not still include Gandhi or Nehru who were still resisting the idea of partition.

Mountbatten Mission

With tensions mounting and with pressures to resolve the growing crisis developing in London, Prime minister Atlee took a major decision. On 20 February 1947, he announced in the House of Commons that it was the "definite intention" of his Government "to take the necessary steps to effect the transference of power to responsible Indian hands by a date not later than June 1948, "and that if unhappily by that date a constitution of an independent India had not been worked out "by a fully representative Constituent Assembly.... His Majesty's Government will have to consider to whom the power of the Central government in British India should be handed over on a due date, whether as a whole to some form of Central Government for British India, or in some areas to the existing provincial governments, or in such a way as may seem most reasonable and in the best interests of the Indian people." At the same time the Prime Minister also announced that Wavell's "wartime appointment" as a Viceroy of India would be ended and that he would be succeeded by Admiral Viscount Mountbatten of Burma.[42]

The announcement was widely hailed in India and in England. Nehru described it as a "wise and courageous" declaration which "not only removes all misconceptions and suspicion but also brings reality and a certain dynamic quality to the present situation in India."[43] Jinnah however refused to endorse the declaration and reiterated his demand for a separate Pakistan. The debates in the British Parliament revealed grave apprehensions of many members as to the consequences of this step. And many spokesmen of the Labour Government admitted that the decision was fraught with grave risks, but they believed that risks were necessary.

Atlee's statement was curious and rather ambiguous. While he had avoided any specific reference to the establishment of Pakistan he had nonetheless left the door open to some sort of a division of the country, since he had clearly stipulated in his statement that in the absence of a Central Government, the British Government would consider transferring power "in some areas to the existing provincial governments."

There was a Central Government in the form of an interim government, but it was really not functioning, because of the deep division between members of the Congress and the Muslim League who had constituted this government. And, it was more than clear that there was indeed no likelihood that the Central Government as it was constituted would be able to function smoothly. So what does Atlee mean? Does it mean that in a number of provinces where the Government had no real control, power would be handed to the provincial governments.? In any event the British position was not very clear.

In the midst of this confusing situation arrived Mountbatten in India on 22 March 1947 with a clear directive from his government that he was to seek, first of all, a solution for united India on the basis of the Cabinet mission plan. But, if in the course of his talks with party leaders, particularly with Jinnah, it became more than apparent that the prospects of an agreed solution on that basis were nil, he must then try to seek an alternative solution.

The only alternative Mountbatten realised was partition. But how to sell this idea to Nehru and Gandhi who were adamantly still against it? How to sell it to the Government at home? How to sell it to soldiers and civil servants who would have the dreadful job of cutting the country in two?

With Gandhi it was not difficult. The Viceroy's clever manoeuvring, after his two meetings with the Mahatma, had already exiled the Mahatma to the periphery of the Congress movement. "He is not a practical man," Mountbatten said in effect to the Congress leaders. "Look at the silly plan he produced to hand India over to Jinnah. This is no time for idealistic gestures-this is the time for action"[44] From this point onwards, the Congress began to take decisions without him. Of course Mountbatten openly and visibly remained very friendly with him giving him all the importance and respect he deserved, but almost excluded Gandhi from all crucial negotiations.

But once Gandhi was neutralised, he turned his attention on Patel who did not need much persuasion, since he had made up his mind. So far as he was concerned, the Muslims could go and take their Muslim majorities with them. Realistic as he was, he saw nothing but trouble ahead if independent India included Muslim League in the Government or in the opposition, thwarting all his plans and rendering the country more and more unstable. The actions of Liaquat Ali Khan as Finance Minister in the Interim Government had given him the fright of his life; for it was Liaquat's budget that had heavily soaked the millionaire backers of Congress, and had shown up the hypocrisy of the Party's claim to be socialist. "As soon as Sardar Patel had been convinced," wrote Azad, "Lord Mountbatten turned his attention to Nehru. Jawaharlal was , at first, not at all willing and reacted violently against the idea of partition, but Lord Mountbatten persisted till Jawaharlal's opposition was torn. Within a month of Lord Mountbatten's arrival in India Jawaharlal, firm opponent of partition, had become, if not a supporter, at least acquiescent towards the idea."[45]

How come a man like Nehru who had violently opposed partition finally accepted it? How come that he accepted the demand of the Muslim League—an organisation for which he had nothing but contempt? What led him to change his mind.? Was it Mountbatten's influence? Was it the charm of his wife with whom he was apparently heavily involved in a sentimental interaction?[46] Or was it the rapidly degenerating situation in north of India where bloody massacres had become the order the day?

It was probably all of them in his astonishing change of front. There were Mountbatten's persuasive arguments that India really had no other choice, there was indeed the charms and sympathy of Lady

Mountbatten who had become linked with the Nehru household; and there was the rising consensus within the Congress in favour of partition that he could not resist. But more than all this, it was what he saw during his travels in the Punjab where violence was rampant, and where massacres had already caused the death of more than 2,000 people. India was rapidly becoming an unholy mess of bloodshed, hatred and brutality; and Nehru was consumed with a sense of powerlessness and hopelessness in the face of all this. A few years before, it may have daunted him and driven him to act. But now he was tired. He felt out of touch with people. Besides, how could he resist the overwhelming pressures that were weighing him down.

In the face of all this he came around to the idea of partition, unhappily and reluctantly. A few days after his visit to the Punjab he went to see Azad. "Jawaharlal asked me in despair," wrote Azad afterwards "what other alternative was there to accepting partition. He recognised that partition was evil, but he held that circumstances were inevitably leading in that direction... and asked me to give up my opposition to partition. He said that it was inevitable, and it would be wisdom not to oppose what was bound to happen. He also said that it would not be wise for me to oppose Lord Mountbatten on this issue."[47]

The Partition

Having obtained successfully the Congress Party's accord, Mountbatten then had to turn his attention to the difficult and dimensional task of actually dividing up the country. That it was indeed the "greatest political and administrative operation in history" is evident from the momentous decisions that had to be taken within two months regarding the apportionment of liabilities and assets, the division of the administrative and armed forces, the alignment of the boundaries between the two countries, etc. The task was gigantic and there wasn't much time left. The armed forces were particularly affected by this decision. "All Indian army officers," declared Claude Auchinleck, the Commander-in-Chief, "hated the idea, but we did what we were told. They had to be split and then all the equipment had to be split with everything else. What it meant was that regiments like my own, half Hindu and half Muslim, were just torn in half—and they wept on each other's shoulders when it happened. It was moving for me and I think it was moving for them. The older officers like myself undoubtedly felt a sense of loss. You felt your life's work would be finished when what you had been working at all along was just torn in two pieces."[48] A number of major decisions had to be taken rapidly in order to come to the end of this gigantic task.

First of all, the exact date of the independence of the two dominions had to be reviewed. Since most of the leaders concerned had accepted the partition plan, and the overall political situation was rapidly degenerating, Mountbatten hastily, and rather thoughtlessly, considered that a rapid and early transfer of power was the only viable way of bringing the situation back to normal. It was therefore decided to advance the date of independence of the subcontinent from June 1948 to 15th August 1947. This was indeed a curious decision—undoubtedly a monumental error. For what India really needed at the time was not an acceleration of the changeover but enough time and determination to bring the rapidly degenerating situation under firm control. Since none of the political parties were really insisting on advancing the date of independence, what was the point of doing so. Nehru told Mountbatten that he was going too fast. Liaquat Ali Khan had gone even further and had declared that he did not believe that under any circumstances, united or divided India could stand on its own legs even by June 1948. Several of the princes too had begged Britain to stay. Even the British officials and most of Mountbatten's staff explicitly opposed any idea he had of leaving India.[49] The Congress, the Muslim League, and what was still the united British administration could have jointly cooperated until June 1948 to bring the situation under control. Besides, it would have given the British Government and the political parties more time to divide up, everything that needed to be divided, and to stop the massacres in the Punjab. Furthermore, even more important, the whole story of partition could have been different; the Hindus could have stayed in Pakistan, while the Muslimswho left to cross the border could have continued to stay in India. Jinnah did not want the Hindus to leave; in fact at the time of the partition he had expressed the hope that populations would not migrate.

Second, a machinery had to be set up to prepare the partition of the subcontinent This was done rapidly. At the apex there was the Partition Committee with Mountbatten as the Chairman, Patel and Rajendra Prasad (later India's first President) representing the Congress, and Liaquat Ali and Sardar Nishtar the League. The committee's function was to coordinate—through a steering committee of two high officials,

Muhammad Ali, a Muslim, and H.M. Patel, a Hindu—the work of a large number of expert committees and sub-committees dealing with everything, from the division of the armed forces, through railways and telegraphs to the duplication of files.

The division of the armed forces, it was decided, was to take place in two stages. The first stage was to consist of a ready operation on a communal basis, followed by an immediate concentration of Muslim majority units in what was going to be Pakistan, and the other units in the rest of the country. The second stage pertained to the voluntary transfer of individuals who wished to join units either in Pakistan or in India. The first stage was carried through with unexpected smoothness. Before the end of June 1947, final decisions had been reached on the Navy and on some units of the Army.

The civil services also had to be divided up and both the British and the Indian members were asked to stay on and help with necessary reconstruction after the transfer of power. The British government guaranteed compensation and pensions, graded according to length of service to British officers, who would be deprived of their careers.

The third major decision pertained to the geographical partition of the country. Which part of the subcontinent was going to opt to which country, and how was this to be done? The decisions were taken by provincial legislative assemblies. They met at the end of June of 1947. Majority of them, which had a Hindu majority, decided to join the new Indian Constituent Assembly. In the case of Bengal and Punjab, where

Muslims were in majority, with Hindus constituting a sizeable minority, the legislative assemblies favoured internal partition. In Bengal the decision was reached in an atmosphere that was relatively free from communal disorder, though tension was only just concealed before the surface. But in the Punjab it was different. There was a daily quota of bomb explosions, fire raising and murders in Lahore, the provincial capital, and Amritsar, the sacred city of the Sikhs. Besides, the Muslim majority areas had voted against the division of the Punjab, as was to be expected, but the non-Muslim areas voted in favour. In Sind, the legislative assembly voted to join Pakistan, a foregone conclusion, and in Baluchistan, a council of tribal chiefs unanimously voted to do the same. In the Muslim majority district of Sylhet, the referendum resulted in a majority favouring Pakistan. Everything seemed to be running smoothly and according to the plan. But there still remained the North-West Frontier Province, where the Congress Party was in power. The referendum was carefully organised by a team of 40 British officers with experience of the Frontier, under a referendum commissioner who was also English. The choice before the electors was either to join Pakistan or India; but in fact there was no choice. For geographical reasons the province could not possibly join India, and for religious reasons the Muslim majority could not join Hindu India.

The verdict was a foregone conclusion. The population obviously voted for Pakistan. But the Red Shirt Movement of the pro-Congress Abdul Gaffar Khan was angling for the alternative to be changed to Pakistan or independence. Even Gandhi thought it was a good idea. But Jinnah would not listen to this "insidious and spurious" demand since his influence had grown immensely after the partition plan had been announced. The referendum passed peacefully in the presence of some 15, 000 troops moved for the occasion. The result was 289,224 votes in favour of Pakistan and only 2,874 in favour of India. Gaffar Khan's movement, which had called its followers to boycott the referendum, had failed, as had failed the Afghan Government, which, in the hope of gaining territory for itself, had strongly supported the idea of independence. In fact, it had sent an official note to the British Government in which it claimed that all the inhabitants of India residing in the West of the Indus river were really afghans, and should therefore be allowed to decide whether they wanted to join Afghanistan. The note was not even acknowledged.

While all this was happening in united India, the Labour Government was busy piloting the Indian Independence Bill through the British Parliament. Passed by the House of Commons on 15th July and by the House of Lords the following day, it received the royal assent on 18th July. "This bill," said Lord Samuel in the House of Lords "is a moral to all future generations. It is a treaty of Peace without a war." Lord Listowel, as Secretary of state for India underlined the significance of the end. "This is a Bill unique in the history of Legislation in the country. Never before such a large portion of world's population achieved complete independence through legislation alone."[50]

Thus after centuries of foreign rule and a country divided against itself, India achieved independence in August 1947. The cost of partition, with all its attendant evils and tragic aftermath still lay in the future. But at the moment it was the time of rejoicing. On the night of 14 August 1947, the Indian Constituent assembly met to usher in the nation's independence. In a moving speech Nehru declared:

"Long years ago we made a tryst with destiny, and now the time comes when we shall redeem our pledge not wholly or in full measure, but very substantially. At the stroke of mid-night hour, when the world sleeps India will wake to life and freedom. A moment comes, which comes but rarely in history, when we step out from the old to the new, when an age ends, and when the soul of the nation long suppressed, finds utterance. It is fitting that at this solemn moment we take the pledge of dedication to the service of India and her people and to the larger cause of humanity."[51]

References

1. Clement Atlee had more than once stated this point.
2. Cited in Alex Von Tunzelmann, *Indian Summer: The Secret History of the End of an Empire* ; London: Simon & Schuster, 2007, p. 121.
3. Patrick French, *Liberty or Death:India's Journey to Independence and division,* New Delhi: Harper Collins 1998.
4. See Peter Clarke, *The Cripps Version: The Life of Sir Stafford Cripps,* London: The Penguin Press, 2001.
5. See Trevor Royle, *The Last Days of the Raj.* London: Coronet Books, 1984.
6. Ibid., p. 112.
7. Denis Dudd, *Jawaharlal Nehru,* Cardiff: University of Wales Press, 1993, p. 35.
8. Ibid., p. 39.
9. For details, see Leonard Mosley, *The Last days of the British Raj,* Bombay: Jaico Publishing House, 1965.

10. Narendra Singh Sarila, *Times of India* 17 March 2000.
11. Alex Von Tunzelmann, op. cit., p.146.
12. Narendra Singh Sarila, *The Shadow of the Great Game: The Untold Story of India's Partition,* New Delhi: Harper-Collins Publishers, 2006, p. 185.
13. Cited in Sikandar Hayat, op. cit. p. 278.
14. For details about his role in India, see Penderel Moon (ed), *Wavell: The Viceroy's Journal,* London: Oxford University Press, 1970.
15. Cited in V.P. Menon, *The Transfer of Power in India,* New Jersey: Princeton University Press, 1957, p. 7.
16. Ibid.
17. Leonard Mosley, op. cit., p. 14.
18. Maulana Abul Kalam Azad, *India Wins Freedom,* Calcutta: Sangam Books Ltd., 1959, p. 143.
19. Ibid. pp. 144-145.
20. Hamayun Mirza, *From Plassey to Pakistan,* Washington: United Press of America Inc, 2001.
21. Ibid.
22. Ibid.
23. Michael Brecher, *Nehru: A Political Biography,* Oxford: Oxford University Press, 1959, p. 121.
24. Ibid.
25. *Harijan,* 16 May 1946.
26. A.G. Noorani, "Cripps and India's Partition," *Frontline* 2 August 2002.
27. Peter Clarke, *The Cripps Version: The Life of Stafford Cripps*, London: Allen Lane, 2001.
28. Leonard Mosley, op. cit.
29. Ibid., 23.
30. Ibid.
31. Ibid.
32. Alex Von Tunzelmann, op. cit., p. 146.
33. Peter Clarke, op. cit.
34. Leonard Mosley, op. cit., p. 70.

35. Ibid., p. 26.
36. *The Statesman,* 5 August 1946.
37. Charles Allen (ed), *Plain Tales From the Raj*, London: Futura Publications Limited, 1975, pp. 253-254.
38. Ibid., p. 254.
39. Jyoti Basu, *The Ones that have lasted: A Political Autobiography*, Calcutta: www. ganeshshakti.com, 1999.
40. Cited in V.P. Menon, op. cit., p. 315.
41. Cited in Leonard Mosley, op. cit., p. 141.
42. Full text in ibid., pp. 506-509.
43. See ibid.
44. Allan Campbell-Johnson, *Mission with Mountbatten,* London: R. Hale, 1952, p. 40.
45. Azad, op.cit., p. 183.
46. Catherine Clément, *Pour l'amour de l'Inde,* Paris: Flammarion, 1993.
47. Azad, op. cit., p. 185.
48. Charles Allen (ed), *Plain Tales From the Raj,* New Delhi: Rupa, 1993, pp. 252-253.
49. Tunzelmann, op. cit., p. 146.
50. Cited in R.P. Masani, op. cit., p. 263.
51. Jawaharlal Nehru *Speeches* Vol. 1, op. cit., p. 25.

PART - II
THE PRESENT

4

Political Democracy

"A billion people in a functioning democracy. Ain't that something."

George Bush 2009

Indian political democracy had its small beginning already under the British. They were the ones who passed laws, established local self-governing institutions, and initiated a sustained political action to govern a dimensional subcontinent. It could hardly have been otherwise since the region they had occupied to constitute an empire was as vast as the continent of Europe, and was almost as faraway as the other end of the planet with a limited British personnel that had crossed the seas to occupy and run India.

The empire-builders, therefore, had no choice but to seek out the natives to govern and to hold the land. They could not possibly run the country with the limited human resources of their own. Besides, it had become historically evident that empires sustained only if the colonial masters were tolerant, and only if they were able to successfully obtain the cooperation of the local residents; otherwise empires come and rapidly disappear. For the British this was possible since they were politically tolerant, technically advanced, and had to reckon with an environment that was not very inimical since most Indians, (Hindus as they were) were discontented with the pitiless governance of the Mughals, and the mercenary dictates of the Portuguese. Besides the other variegated Indian governing dynasties that were teetering in the face of intramural disputes and growing conflicts contributed to some degree of openness to the British.

British Process of Self- Governance

All this British process of self- governance was spawned with the proclamation of Indian Councils Act of 1892 under which the principle of elections was introduced for the first time in Indian history—a principle that was applied to the ten established Legislative Councils, one of which was located at the centre while the nine others were set up in the big provinces of India. All of these councils were slowly enlarged in Indian membership and were attributed broadening powers including a voice in the setting up of the budget of the year and the right to put questions to the executive council. Also there were, by the turn of the 19th century, as many as 700 municipalities most of whom were composed of Indians representing a total population of more than 17 million.[1]

All this process must not be underestimated. For inaugurating—howsoever limited—the practice of hiring Indians for bureaucratic positions, and of electing them to legislatures and municipalities was a dual process that generated considerable experience of monitoring and deciding even if it was at a lower level.

The process was accelerated under the Montague-Chelmsford reforms (1919) granting self-governing institutions by stages, the most important aspect of which was the institutionalisation of a fairly elaborated diarchic system in the provinces with the Governors possessing the responsibilities of finance and law and order, while the other subjects (public health, education, public works, etc.) were operated by a parliamentary government with different ministers placed in-charge of different subjects.

The self rule reached a peak with the Government of India Act of 1935 under which partial elections were held with Indians of different hues participating in the polls,including the Congress and the Muslim League. This was the first occasion when direct elections were conducted in the provinces with the Congress majority forming ministries in most of the provinces with the Congress leaders as chief ministers. Govind Vallabh Pant, one of the major Congress luminaries in the UP province, for example, was nominated as the head of the government who held the post between 1937 to 1939. But, it was not only in UP. It was all over the country. If it was not the Congress, it was the other Indians leaders belonging to the regions.

It is important to note that Hindi was declared as the official language in the Congress controlled provinces, and the Congress flag was given the status of a national flag. That this was one of the most remarkable electoral experiences is evident from the important fact that large quantum of Indians were involved in the politics of day-to-day governance without any interference from the Governors in the legislative affairs of the provinces. In fact the Congress made a major issue on this point by declaring that it would not set up its government until the British Government agreed to its demand that the Governor would not use his powers in legislative affairs. Many discussions took place between the Congress and the British Government and at last the British Government consented to the Congress demand.

Government of India Act proved to be a major landmark in the development of India. For all its 'ifs' and 'buts', its complications and hesitations, it marked a point of no-return in constitutional development,

If one were to add to all this the important fact that one third of the total Indian area and one fifth of the population of the Empire were ruled by Indian princes, who made their own laws, levied their own taxes, and appointed their own officials and judges.

Self-governance thus had already reached a dimensional stage before the British left India.

Lasting for more than fifty years, the whole process of governance had resulted in the emergence and the proliferation of countless self-governing institutions all over the subcontinent making it possible for large segments of Indians—including the organised oppositions—to gain the difficult experience of governance.

Consider the importance of this phenomenon. Though severely limited to those actively involved in the process, it was nonetheless a masterly act of self-governance whose ramifications could only be beneficial to the country.

While the efficacious operationalisation of this process was one way of managing and governing a vast land, it was also, for many British proponents an act of normative faith in the system of consultations and elections. For the framers of the reforms "the gradual development of self-governing institutions" was "an act of faith." They firmly believed that through the experience of votes the Indians will learn, over a period of time, the effective power of voting. "The rural voter," argued the proponents, "will find himself cajoled or bought or coerced into voting in a way that does him no good. But, eventually it will dawn upon him, as it has done upon the agricultural classes elsewhere, that because he has a vote he has a means of protecting himself, and that if those who claim to represent him neglect his interests, he can discard them."[2]

This type of thinking and mind-set, among the segments of British reforming elite underpinned the Indian evolution towards some form of democratic rule even if it was limited. But, there was another important element in this process—an element of growing pressure that was exercised by the Indian National Congress for the continuous expansion of the system of governance expressing openly its dissatisfaction at the slowness of the whole process.

It is important to note that while the Congress party was the leading proponent of self rule, it abandoned this incremental elective process when the Motilal Nehru Committee , appointed, by an "all-party conference", published a report in 1929 that demanded a great leap to "Dominion Status" as "the next immediate step."[3] His son, Jawaharlal Nehru, went even further at the session of the Congress party in 1929 in Lahore where he demanded unequivocally complete independence of India.

It was thus the combined pressure, emanating from segments of British proponents favouring the expansion of self-rule, and the public insistence by the Congress (until 1929) for its acceleration that resulted in the endemic expansion of the elective system.

That all this was indeed evident from the fact that India became well equipped in governance with the emergence of Indian personnel at all levels at the time of the independence of the country—undoubtedly an historic landmark that was able to effectively steer from the tumultness of the partition of the subcontinent.

The other dimension in this ongoing process was environmental. While the British, on the one hand, had a record of repression, imprisonment, and forced silencing of expression during critical periods of Indian colonial history, there were, on the other hand, long periods of British rule that permitted the freedom of speech and the unhindered functioning of the media against imperialism. This was, in effect, an institutional transplantation of what they had established in their own country —a transplantation that made it possible for the nationalists to denounce the government, for the media to express all sorts of opinions, and for the publishing houses to produce "subversive" literature, including the ones that were imported from Bolshevik Russia.

The third dimension in this ongoing democratic process was atmospheric—atmospheric in the sense that the nationalist opposition had acquired a mind-set of liberty, and a feeling of fearlessness from the occupying colonial power. India, of course, was not independent, but the atmosphere of unabashed ideological dauntlessness that prevailed in the country was due to the system that had been established in the country.

While, in all authoritarian regimes in the thirties of the last century, (Bolshevik Russia, Nazi Germany Fascist Italy and Spain) the atmosphere of fearlessness was absent it would hardly have been possible to transplant it to their colonies. Nations, in sum, do not transplant a different atmosphere elsewhere from what they have in their own countries.

Consider, on the other hand, colonial India. The British could hardly have transplanted an authoritarian atmosphere in the colonial areas which was alien to what they had in their own country. Admittedly there were periods of authoritarianism, and repression, but that were present only during periods of crises. Consider all the ideas that were freely floating around India. Think of all what the Indians could read, write and express, all the travelling they could do, all the conferences they could attend, all the broadsides they could direct at imperial Britain etc. And, think of the political prisons where Indian nationalists were herded together; their prison lives hardly resembled a prison in the strict sense of the word since the element of British leniencies were considerable. And lastly consider the Indians living in

England and studying in British universities. They constituted the front rank of the intellectuals who returned to India carrying "subversive" ideas.

All the three British aspects (institutional, environmental and atmospheric) are thus the legacies that London left in India, and which are present to this day.

What is Democracy ?

If one were to accept the thesis that political democracy is really "a mechanism of appointing and removing governments through majority rule,"[4] and a "method of taking political decisions, of compromising and reconciling conflicting interests,"[5] then the British had laid the basis, though very partial, of such a system during colonial rule. Admittedly, it was not a complete "mechanism" since India was a part of the empire; but the very fact that controlled self-government and restricted voting procedure was put in place, the British had transplanted their own system onto India—along with the environmental and atmospheric aspects of political democracy.

All the three legacies have continued to flourish in post-independent India. They have been fully expanded, and do not contain any of the restraints that characterised British rule. The mechanism of political democracy was carried to its logical conclusion by the elimination of all the electoral restraints. The mechanism of appointing and removing governments through majority rule was firmly established; the freedom of expression and action was guaranteed, and was compounded with the maintenance of an atmosphere of fearlessness and free thinking. "Obviously", declared

Jawaharlal Nehru on 13 December 1946, while moving the objective resolution of the constitution :

> We are aiming at democracy and nothing less than a democracy. What form of de-mocracy, what shape it might take is another matter. The democracies of the present day, many of them in Europe and elsewhere, have played a great part in the world's progress. Yet it may be doubtful If those democracies may not have to change their shape somewhat before long if they have to remain completely democratic. We are not going just to copy, I hope, a certain democratic procedure or an institution of a so-called democratic country. We may improve upon it. In any event whatever system of government we may establish here must fit in with the temper of our people and be acceptable to them. We stand for democracy, it will be for this house to determine what shape to give to that democracy, the fullest democracy.[6]

The Indian constitution, freely debated and consensually agreed upon, all the basic principles and objectives of political democracy: the proclamation of universal adult suffrage, the freedom of expression, the dispersal of political power through marked separation of the judiciary, the legislature and the executive, and the explicit acceptance of a majority rule through the alternative establishment of variegated governments after a free and unimpeded consultation of its constituents. To this must be added the establishment of a congenial environmental atmosphere of fearlessness of the people in the country.

However, notwithstanding all the post-independent tumultuousness that India had to face after the partition of the subcontinent, and after the proclamation of a violent upheaval by the Communist Party of India, the country was nonetheless able to establish a free pluralistic institutionalised system after the independence of the country—a pluralistic system that was additionally composed of countless autonomous groups, societies institutions, etc., that operated freely without any control by the State.

All that had been stipulated in the constitution had to be of course carried out faithfully. But what was equally important was (a) the existence of an appropriate leadership to effectively carry out the democratic task, (b) the palpable establishment of institutional safeguards to freely conduct the electoral system.

The Indian leadership was committed to a public philosophy that embodied the values of democracy, for they cannot be, as argued by Walter Lippman, "made to work except by men who possess the philosophy in which democracy was conceived and founded."[7]

Much earlier, John Stuart Mill was even more explicit. In fact, he had argued that it is not only the leadership, but the people as a whole who subscribed to this philosophy. He wrote:

A people may prefer a free government, but if from indolence and carelessness, or cowradices, or want of public spirit, they are unequal to the exertions necessary for preserving it, if they will not fight for it when directly attacked, if they can be deluded by the article used to teach them out of it; if by momentary discouragement or temporary panic, or fit of enthusiasm for an individual they can be induced to lay their liberties at the feet of a great man in all these cases they are more or less unfit for liberty: and although it may be for their good to have had even for a short time, they are unlikely to enjoy it.[8]

While the Indian people may not have had great faith in political democracy at the beginning of Indian independence, the leadership was deeply committed to the establishment of the pluralistic system. While political giants like Gandhi, Nehru, Patel and Prasad, etc., had gone through the bitter experience of repression and imprisonment, they were, all of them, clear proponents of democratic rule. Political disagreements were common amongst them on a wide array of issues, but not on political democracy. On this they all agreed.

The institutional safeguards, after independence, were provided with the establishment of an election commission as the independent constitutional authority whose task was to assure free elections. While in the initial stages it performed an administrative role with only one election commissioner, it has, through the years, become an independent constitutional authority with three commissioners who were finally given a status equivalent to that of a supreme court judge who enjoys office for six years or up to 65 years of age, whichever is earlier. It is important to note that the chief election commissioner can only be removed after impeachment by the Parliament.[9]

The free electoral experience of more than sixty years has proved, according to Krishnamurthy, that electoral management is marked by "complete transparency at the time of nomination, holding of elections, as well as declaration of results. At the time of nomination, candidates need to file copies of affidavits containing information, such as educational qualifications, assets and liabilities, dependent family members, record of criminal convictions and pending cases in court and, outstanding dues to the government."[10]

It would seem that perhaps nowhere in the world such comprehensive background information of contesting candidates is available to voters at the time of elections.[11]

When one looks at the political panorama of the last sixty years, India has had elections at all levels—elections that are free and institutionally controlled and monitored by an independent electoral commission.

All the general elections that have been conducted in the country have been consensually considered as free by political participants within the country and international observers from without.

What could be a greater symbol and greater proof of the free electoral process than the important fact that of the fifteen prime ministers, who have so far governed the country, almost half of them belong to non-congress parties. At the state level the change of the guards was even more frequent and even more rampant, so much so that India has had and has Communists and other opposition party leaders as chief ministers duly elected by the electoral process.

The third institutional dimension in this electoral process is the establishment of the *panchayat raj* at the grass roots level. *Panchayat* literally means assembly (*yat*) of five (*panch*) wise and respected elders and chosen and accepted by the village community. While this process had begun pragmatically it was institutionalised in April 1993 by a constitutional amendment that explicitly provided a 3-tier system under which (a) elections are held every five years, and (b) under which the principal focus is on development.[12] The electoral process begins at the village and continues at the "block" and district levels.

The 3-tier system has brought the democratic process to the grass roots level—a level which has generated considerable interest among the rural poor since such an institution is directly linked to their real problems—much more than at the national and provincial levels. While it is still unclear regarding its workability, the country has consensually accepted its role in the whole electoral process. While there have been attempts to insulate village politics from the parties, it is generally viewed as unrealistic in a country that has chosen political democracy as its model where political parties underpin the whole political system.[13]

The politics of free and regular consultations have thus been firmly institutionalised in the country. With more than sixty years of such an experience, it is hardly anymore possible—in fact inconceivable—for any mainstream political party to transgress what has indeed become a secular trend. Consider the brief period of authoritarian rule when an emergency was imposed by Indira Gandhi. The clamping down on the established political system was consensually opposed by most of the population. And at the first electoral opportunity for its removal was seized that resulted in the humiliating defeat of its proponent, Indira Gandhi. That she had herself realised that authoritarian system really had no future in the country indicates the broad cosensuality of political democracy.

The Indian model is comparable to the system in the West. What is perhaps even more remarkable is that the Indian political system of free electoral consultations preceded the industrialisation of the country ; whereas in the West the free electoral process emerged only after industrialisation had been effectuated. All the problems and difficulties that accompany industrial growth, therefore, had in effect been met before the political revolution in Europe, whereas in India it was the other way around: political revolution has preceded industrialisation thus making the whole process of development much more difficult and much more problematic.

Industrialisation is not only a technical advancement of the economy, it is also the cobbling and adaptation of the social order that accompanies the change. Naturally, it is politically easier for the decision makers to successfully grapple with the social disorders as the population is not equipped with the democratic instruments to frustrate the task of the leaders.

The institutional framework of a pluralist democracy is thus well established and consensually respected. It is hard to belie.

Liberalism

Political democracy has another dimension—the dimension of liberalism. Classically it was considered a doctrine for determining what governments should do and what they should not do— in effect determining the limits of the government. "Liberalism," as Hayek put it, "is a doctrine what the law ought to be, democracy a doctrine about the manner of determining what will be the law."[14]

In sum, the classicist argument is that the pursuit of liberty is in effect incompatible with the pursuit of equality, since the pursuit of equality can only operate successfully with the establishment of a big government, with the emergence of oligarchy, and with the collateral decline of liberalism. Liberalism in the words of Harold Laski, has "always taken a negative attitude to social action....and "has accordingly tended to make an antithesis (as a rule an unconscious one) between liberty and equality." It has furthermore discovered "a system of fundamental rights which the State is not entitled to invade."[15]

The inflation of this process in UK over the past century is best illustrated by A.J.P. Taylor's remark that "until August 1914 a sensible English man could pass through life and hardly notice the existence of the state beyond the post office and the police man."[16]

While the original classical argument that the onset of "mass democracy" and the "pursuit of equality" may end up in some form of authoritarianism may have some logical relevance, the fact of the matter is that with the passage of time, compounded with the growing material needs of the people, have unavoidably resulted in the establishment of bigger and bigger governments.

For the classicists this would inevitably result in the decline of freedom. "For two hundred years," declared George Orwell, "we had sawed and sawed and sawed and sawed at the branch we were sitting on. And in the end, much more suddenly than anyone had foreseen, our efforts were rewarded and down we came. But, unfortunately there had been a little mistake, The thing at the bottom was not a bed of roses after all, but a cesspool full of barbed wire."[17]

All this process of striving for greater equality actually began with the European social democrats in the nineteenth century when states and governments, having became all powerful, resulted in social democratic determination to focus on the amelioration of the material lives of people.

While years of social democratic initiatives did result in societal improvement, second thoughts began to emerge regarding the continuation of state action. For one thing the amelioration process was no more ongoing under the aegis of the welfare state. It had certainly served its purpose but was no more perceived as an efficacious instrument in improving the lives of the people. For another, the welfare state had generated a vast powerful bureaucracy and an excessively regulated society, the net result of which was, in the eyes of many observers, the contraction of political democracy and the abandonment of most individual initiatives.

While many did not see the logic of this argumentation, there was nonetheless the emergence of some innovative thinking. A new "third way" was proposed between neo-liberalism and classical social democracy—a way that advocated a "new mixed economy" that would constitute a viable synergy between private and public sectors.[18]

The Indian Model

India, on the other hand, has continued on the path of making the state a powerful instrument in the sustainable growth of Indian economy—an option that had resulted in the further nationalisation of industries, and the firm establishment of the so-called "license Raj" under which hardly any initiative could be taken in the economic sector without the explicit approval of a vast and powerful bureaucracy.

This expansive and invasive intrusion had spilled over to other sectors, including education, social services, etc., hardly leaving any major initiative to the private sector.

One of the worst ramifications of this system was the massive emergence of uncontrollable corruption among the bureaucrats who looked upon this newly found and spacious power as an opportunity to make material gain. The quantum of people lining up in the corridors of power to seek licenses or permits to expand their affairs had indeed become dimensional.

Finally, in the nineties of the 20th century some let up had to be introduced to this on-going and highly regulative phenomenon, in the face of a crumbling and tanking Indian economy.[19]

However, notwithstanding the continuous expansiveness of the regulatory power of the state in practically all the sectors, it is worthy to note that the Indian political model has amply demonstrated that the free mechanism of electoral politics was not affected. It continued to function freely. While the original classicists were perhaps not too far wrong in their original philosophical and political argumentation that free scope of the individual does get restrained by the regulatory power of the state, their fear, on the other hand, that free functioning of political democracy would be actually undermined in the process does not correspond with the political evolution of democratic states. The increased power of the state and the mechanism of alternative governments are not mutually exclusive. They can co-exist as is the case in most democratic states. India does not really have a credible alternative.

But, on the other hand, it cannot be denied that the expanding and highly regulatory power of the welfare state blemishes the actual functioning of political democracy and severely hems in the free action of the individual. While this is unavoidable, the Indian political system would have to continuously assure itself that a balance is maintained and that welfarism does not excessively intrude into the free life of the individual.

Drawbacks of Indian Democracy

Nonetheless, there are a host of specific Indian factors, characteristics and circumstances that restrain the free functioning of Indian democracy. Undeniably, India is one of the world's most unequal societies in which social inequality revolves around the axes of class, caste, tribal status, religion and gender. All this is heavily visible all over the country. You cannot escape it.

First of all most of rural India is illiterate and poor. While it may not hinder rural Indians from understanding their day-to–day problems—even more so than the educated classes—they may not be able to translate them into macro issues on which national and even regional elections are invariably held.

Such being the case, one wonders if the level of manipulation by politicians does not become high at the national level.

Manipulation, of course, is universal. It is everywhere, including the developed countries. But manipulation among the developed countries is hardly comparable to the one that exists in India where it is optimised by Indian poverty and illiteracy. Consider all that manipulation can do in pushing the Indian constituents in a given electoral direction with money. While it has become very much a part of the Indian system, visible all over the country, it manifests itself particularly during the time of elections.

Add to this the caste system. While it may have originally performed a useful societal function, it has, through the centuries, become one of the greatest social evils "plaguing India today."[20] It is undeniable that Indian electoral politics is heavily governed by caste vote banks. When the time comes to select candidates for elections, practically most—if not all— parties invariably choose appropriate candidates which have a numerical caste distribution since it is well-known that votes in most areas are cast on caste lines. It has become one of the weighty factors in electoral behaviour. Hardly any political party can escape this dimension. To take only a recent example, consider Mayawati, the chief minister of UP. Her elections to the responsibility of power can be attributed to biased caste politics in the state. Notwithstanding her known corruptibility, much of which has already surfaced in the media, she remains one of the most powerful politicians in the country; so much so that she was being projected as one of the serious candidates for the prime ministership of the country. Though this has happily not taken place in 2009 elections, who knows what will happen in the future.

While the electoral panorama all over the country has indeed been transformed by the political emergence of hitherto deprived castes, it is a breakthrough that has nonetheless severely distorted electoral politics, since voting is solidly cast on caste lines.

Another example of the biased nature of Indian electoral politics is the Hindu traditional tendency of lionizing those who happen to be leaders. There is this general and persistent hinduist belief that those who happen to be leaders embody and represent exceptionally high values. Where else do we find this strange phenomenon of seeking and obtaining satisfaction by simply looking at the leaders, thus experiencing what the Hindus call "Darshan"—a sort of a spiritual happiness. Look at the myriad pictures of rural poor sitting with folded hands at the feet of the master or even from afar obtaining some strange spiritual contentment. How much does this "spirituality" numerically affects electoral behaviour, it is of course difficult to say, but the fact that it is very much there can hardly be ignored in any analysis of Indian electoral behaviour.

The religious dimension is equally important in electoral politics. The different communities are heavily influenced in their voting behaviour. The Bharatiya Janata Party (BJP), the second major grouping in the country, clearly is Hinduist in orientation. While, there are some signs, among small liberal segments of the party, that Muslim electorate vote should not be completely ignored, the broad consensus has clearly opted for *Hindutva* strategy. It did not put up a single Muslim candidate in the Uttar Pradesh and Gujarat elections in 2007 perhaps because it was unlikely to get a large chunk of their votes or because it can do without it. The Indian National Congress, the largest party in the country and officially secular in character, is no better. While it cajoles them at election time, it barely gives them tickets.[21]

Institutional Obstacles

There are furthermore a host of institutional problems that distort or weaken political democracy. There is, first of all, a considerable proliferation of candidates for all elections. While this may be a sign of the vibrancy of the system, it has an adverse effect: winning candidates do not get more than 15 to 25 per cent of the votes polled. Consider the Lok Sabha elections of 2004. Almost sixty per cent of the members of the parliament were elected on minority votes. At the provincial election it is even more pronounced, since the vote turnout is lower than in the national elections. There is therefore a "need for the immediate review of the existing system in the country."[22]

Proportional Representation (PR) could be a credible alternative way of electing candidates since most, if not all parties, would have a voice in governance. But to accommodate PR "the basic structure of the constitution may require fundamental changes, since the cabinet system with a ceremonial president proceeds on a different jurisprudential foundation."[23]

Besides, the unavoidable proliferation of political parties, and the collateral representation in the legislative bodies, under such a system, would only generate greater instability which India can hardly afford, given its already enhanced political uncertainties. Add to this, the emergence of coalitional politics, already endemic at the centre and the provinces, stability of the country would be further endangered.

Since a number of years, it is, furthermore, no more possible for political parties to have clear majorities in the Parliament. The ones who were once powerful in mainstream Indian politics now have to seek out other national and/or regional parties to establish national or regional governments. While this system has become more representative, it has also become more unstable, leading to weak leaderships and incoherent policies with a clear proliferation of competitive candidates who are striving to head a central or provincial governments.

This is perhaps the most striking and most dramatic transformation of the Indian political system—a transformation that is becoming an integral part of Indian politics—with which India will have live with and work with almost permanently.

Declining leadership

The broad definition of successful leadership, to risk a generalisation, contains six basic components: (a) possessing a broad but clear vision of what it wishes to achieve; (b) manifesting a charismatic ability of motivating people to act towards achieving a common goal proclaimed by the leadership; (c) recognising and managing the resources at its disposal; (d) exhibiting a persistent capacity of communicating and inspiring; (e) closely supervising initiatives launched and actions taken and (f) showing a capacity of getting people or groups of people to do something they don't want to do.

With the possible exception of nationalists icons like Gandhi, Nehru, Patel, Azad, etc., who fit into the definitional framework of leadership, and who played a weighty role in transiting India to independence, much of the "macro-political" leadership thereafter did not fit into the proposed framework. If anything it had, through the years, declined morally and politically with endemic corruption rampant all over the country and with the level of intramural disputes, intrigues, including an obsessive search for power, having ratcheted up considerably. Besides, the growing establishment of coalition governments in Indian politics, both nationally and regionally, have made the emergence of real leadership even more problematic since the leaders have to devote a considerable amount of their time and energy constructing governments founded on a host of compromises where leadership is much less required than the art of negotiations. Furthermore, the imagery of the Indian leadership is continuously declining; so much so that it has become a secular trend in the country

The salt thus is being slowly wiped off the peanuts pushing the system into a continuous state of declination and exacerbation. The effective functioning of political democracy is no more only dependent on institutional safeguards, including the adequate dispersal of systemic power; it is also very much dependent on and underpinned by morality, integrity and incorruptibility of those who lead and those who populate the system. For, howsoever effective the institutional safeguards may be firmly installed, and howsoever general may be the consensus regarding the vibrancy of the pluralistic system, it will get hopelessly gridlocked by the absence of integrity among those who govern the system.

Adverse Ramifications of Political Democracy

Political democracy has also generated a host of political problems. While they would have surfaced under any system, it tends to aggravate them rendering them overwhelmingly egregious.

While political pluralism has the blessings of openness and the benefit of general endorsement within the country, it is slow in action, divisive in concurrence, and sluggish in operation. The whole process is underpinned by dissonance with a widening and time-consuming gap between decisions codified and their implementation.

While democracy everywhere is blemished by ambivalence and torpidity, it is more so in India where slothfulness abounds, and where pluralistic culture is less rooted than in the western world.

The ramifications of all this is that India suffers from administrative slackness and political divisiveness and is generating considerable languidity.

India thus is confronted with a series of turmoils—turmoils that are difficult to resolve. The system surfaces the dissent and weaknesses where consensus is required; it generates incoherence where fixed determination is needed; and it encourages a level of violence where peace is essential. No less than 2611 Indians have died in the eruption of different types of violences, including terrorism, discontent in Kashmir, and ethnic upsurge in north-eastern parts of the country.[24]

Consider India's territorial integrity. It is challenged by a virtual civil war in its north-eastern parts, by China in the north, and by Pakistan in the northwest. None of these intractable issues have been resolved, and the likelihood of their denouement are as remote as ever.

Furthermore what about the ongoing violent Maoist upheavals within the country. While Prime Minister Manmohan Singh had admitted that this was one of the major insecurities that is threatening India, the crass inability of the government to contain it is very much evident.

Think of the emergence of Islamic fundamentalism and right wing *Hindutva* in the country . Without going into all the details of their origins, radical religious bipolarity has become a major threat to peace and stability within the country. In effect, the country is becoming divided with 80 million Muslims severely alienated from the Indian mainstream. While the ongoing rise of *Hindutva* all over the country has aggravated the process of religious bipolarity, the original alienation, it must be admitted, that it was spawned by the Muslims themselves many of whom are striving to remain distant by insisting on maintaining their own separate civil code and by insisting on maintaining *Madrasas* (schools) where quoranic code is the centre of education[25].

Consider the disquieting emergence of Islamic fundamentalism on India's western flank—a fundamentalism that is effectively challenging the very integrity of existing states. What is happening on India's immediate western flank (Pakistan and Afghanistan) is even worse where the two countries are increasingly unable to face the growing threat. India indeed has become the greatest victim of Islamic fundamentalism, the most important manifestation of which are regular terrorist attacks in the country. The quantum of such violence is far greater in India than anywhere else on the planet, the most violent being the one that exploded in the heart of Mumbai in November 2008 with more than 200 hundred brutally assassinated.

And finally consider the emergence of massive corruption at all levels within the country. While corruption is universal, there is perhaps no country—not even China—which has reached such a pivotal level as India. It has become a part of Indian culture. The level of manoeuvrability is so endemic that it allows unprecedented corruptible initiatives of which one reads and hears practically every day.

While all these blemishments may have surfaced under any system, one could validly ask the question if the mechanism of democracy and its collateral defects have not contributed to their aggravation.

The purpose of this exercise of highlighting the dark side of the democratic system is not so much to recommend its rejection as to show how far political democracy can go in its blemishment, if it is unregulated by the absence of strict laws, if it is institutionally unrestrained by moral turpitude, and if is governed by flawed leadership.

In any event, even if all these defects were to be removed, the institutional mechanism of democracy, inherently underpinned by dissonance and divisiveness, will always generate some problem or the other.

In sum, to risk a generalisation, it could be suggested that the continuous maintenance of pluralist democracy reposes on three basic factors. For one thing it is historical. For almost more than sixty years the empire builders had established incrementally a system of self rule—a system that had given the country the experience of governance. Large segments of Indians, hailing from all walks of life, including the nationalists, were exposed to the difficult task of ruling and decision making. For another, this long experience had generated a habit, "The aptitude of democracy," argued George F. Kennan "is not something that is born into people. It comes, alas only from experience, from long encounters with reality. To be useful, you have to gain the quality of habit"[26] —a quality to which Indians have fixated themselves by the time the country had become independent. And lastly, a whole series of institutionally imperative safeguards had been injected into the constitution and into the Indian legislation to effectively maintain the operation of pluralistic society.

It must be recognised that while democracy may well be perceived as ineffective in its functionality, and sluggish in its activities pertaining to social change, there is hardly any superior system to replace it.

Rudyard Kipling's famous axiom "Oh the East is East and the West is West and never the twain shall meet" may have some relevance to the cultural gap that separated the colonisers from the colonised, but the twain, on the other hand do meet, when it comes to political institutions. For sixty years of independence have bound all Indians, rich and poor, to a single commitment: political democracy.

References

1. Self-rule growing in British India, *New York Times,* 4 June 1916.
2. *Report on Indian Constitutional Reform 1918*, Delhi : Deep Publications, 1977, pp. 93-94.
3. Asiatic Society of Bangladesh, *Constitutional Development Dhaka,* 1991.
4. Robert Moss, *The Collapse of Democracy*, London: Abacuss, 1977, p. 11.
5. E.M.F. Dublin, *The Politics of Democratic Socialism,* London: Routledge 1945, p. 271.
6. Extract from a speech delivered by Jawaharlal Nehru, op. cit.
7. Walter Lippman, *The Public Philosphy*, New York: Little Brown 1955, p. 60-61.
8. John Stuart Mill, *Considerations on a Representative Government*, New York : Harper and Brothers, 1862, p. 11.
9. For details, see T.S, Krishnamurthy. *The Miracle of Democracy: India's Amazing Journey,* New Delhi: HarperCollins, 2008.
10. Ibid., 131.
11. Ibid.
12. Panchati Raj, *Wikiepedia, the Free Encyclopedia,* 6 March 2009.
13. For some discussion on the subject see Myron Weiner, "Political Parties and Panchayati Raj", in S.P. Aiyar and

R Srinivasan, (edited), *Studies in Indian Democracy,* New Delhi:Allied Publishers Private Limited, 1965.

14. F.A Hayek, *The Constitution of Liberty,* London: Routledge, 1960, p. 103.
15. Harold J. Laski, *The Rise of Liberalism. The Philosphy of a Business Civilization,* New York: Harper and Brothers, 1936, p. 2.
16. A.J.P. Taylor, *English History 1914-1945*, Oxford: Oxford University Press, 1965, p. 1.
17. George Orwell, "Notes on the Way," *Collected Essays, Journals and Letters,* London: Penguin 1871, Vol. 2, p. 30.
18. See Anthony Giddens, *The Third Way: The Renewal of Social Democracy,* Cambridge: Politiy Press, 1998.
19. For details see chapter V.
20. Markandey Katju, "Look back on the caste system," *New Age Weekly,* 1-7 February 2009.
21. See Zoya Hasan, :*Politics of Inclusion: Castes, Minorities and Affirmative Action,* New Delhi:Oxford University Press, 2009.
22. T. S. Krishnamurthy, op.cit., p. 53.
23. V.K. Krishna Iyer, "Democracy in the election process,"*The Hindu,* 4 July 2007.
24. *Le Monde* 21 April 2009.
25. For details regarding the status of Muslims, see Wendy Kristianasen, "Plongée au Coeur de L'Inde Musulmane," *Le Monde Diplomatique,* January 2009.
26. George F. Kennan, *At a Century's Ending : Reflections 1982-1995,* London: W.W.Norton and Company 1996, p. 176.

5

Mutating Economy

Economic Development in its simplest form is the creation of economic wealth for all citizens within the diverse layers of society so that all people have access to potential increased quality of life, job creation, economic output and increased taxable basis are the most common measurement tools.

Peter's Business and Economy issues 2006

India's development strategy can be broadly divided into two phases. The first spanning over three decades— after the independence of the country in 1947—was essentially an inward looking plan of action whose normative goal was to establish a self-reliant, self-sustaining, and socialistically-oriented economy to meet the needs of a large and growing internal market— a market whose potential was perceived as gigantic given the country's dimensional population.

The second strategy, timidly introduced in the mid-eighties but formally proclaimed in 1991, was just the opposite with a focus on expanding private investments, constructing an inter-dependent and export-oriented economy with a wide window opened to the outside world. In sum moving towards globalisation.

THE FIRST PHASE

Though, during the first phase, India had by no means cut itself off from the outside world—and is hardly comparable to the autarkical communist growth models— it nonetheless was firmly of the opinion that neither trade nor market-oriented economy nor even capital inflows were considered crucial for the expansion of the economy. The maintenance of autonomy, shielded from the vicissitudes of the global fluctuating market-oriented economies, was perceived as the only sound way of achieving an all-round economic system that was suitable to India.

Such a broad development strategy was based on three considerations.

The first was ideological. Having opted for what was generally termed as a "socialistic pattern of society,"[1] the prevalent consensual Indian perception was that such a normative goal could be credibly reached only through a firm politics of self-reliance. The socialist imprint on those who were at the helm of affairs was indeed overwhelming. In fact, it had become an indelible part of the nationalist rhetoric already in the thirties when many mainstream Indian leaders were enamoured by the Soviet experiment. But, it was one of those much bandied words which was never given a palpable content by any one of them. The term was like a "weak and hollow reed in which one could blow any kind of music."[2] For Gandhi it was a "beautiful word" whose origins could arguably be traced to ancient Hindu scriptures, and whose meaning for him was that "all the members of the society are equal—none low none high."[3] For Jawaharlal Nehru socialism was "not merely an economic doctrine...but a vital creed which I hold with all my head and heart."[4] A little later he defined socialism as "the socialisation of vacuum,"[5] which in effect amounted to the concentration of public investments in selected areas free from private enterprise—a mode of thinking and belief very different from the classical Marxist concept which believed in the actual taking over of the means of production. To the Indian National Congress, Nehru's party, the socialistic pattern of society was not only the "socialisation of vacuum". It was much more. It was envisioned as a system "where the principal means of production are under social leadership or control, production is speeded, and there is an equitable distribution of wealth."[6]

The measure of incoherence regarding the whole concept can be discerned from the way attempts were made to postulate contradictory thinking into one stream of thought. Though the Indian normative goal of establishing a socialistic society was originally influenced by the Fabian school of thought, many Indians, including Nehru, were also attracted by the Soviet pattern of planning—clearly a very antithetical position, and clearly a reflection of the confusion that reigned in Indian ideological thinking.

Nevertheless, despite all the ambiguities surrounding the concept of socialism, and despite the different meanings attributed to the definition, it was repeatedly proclaimed by practically all the mainstream political leaders that socialism, in effect, was India's major goal, and that credible modernisation was possible only within that ideological framework. It is indeed striking how isolated, and how few were the dissident political voices that thought differently.

The second consideration was political. Heavily determined by nationalism, it was generally believed by the Indian decision makers that excessive economic interaction with the developed countries would make India unavoidably too dependent on powerful manipulative external forces—clearly an unacceptable situation for a country that had just gained independence, and that had consensually opted for the policy of nonalignment. The asymmetrical pattern of international economic relations had clearly argued against any excessive interaction with the dominant international economic system since the dangers of absorption in the global economy were perceived as dangerously real. The core-periphery theories expounded by many political scientists—and convincingly demonstrated by Terrance K. Hopkins, Immanuel Wallerstein and associates[7] with solid historical evidence—had much to do with Indian reluctance to build up excessive interaction with expansionist market-oriented economies. The relational pair of core and periphery was being extensively used internationally at the time when India was shaping its development strategy.[8]

The third consideration was economic. For a developing country like India, ran the Indian argumentation, international trade could hardly be an engine of growth since the "deteriorating terms of trade" for agricultural and mineral products had become a secular trend between the developed and developing countries[9] with no hope of any real change for years to come. As Indian exports were essentially composed of primary commodities, the inelasticity of demand would limit their absorption by the international market. Indian planners, therefore, argued that it is "only after industrialisation has proceeded some way that increased productivity will reflect in large export earnings."[10]

An import substitution policy was thus viewed as the only viable solution for the country—a solution, it was argued, that would open the prospects of rapid all-round development on the line that India would like to follow.

India had thus rejected the two existing growth models that dominated the international system—the one communist-oriented autarkical model and the other capitalistic export-oriented approach—and had poised itself for a middle-of the-road development strategy under the aegis of what Chalmers Johnson had termed as the "developmental state."[11]

It is important to note that the original developmental strategy was based on a very broad national consensus within the country. Practically all the mainstream political parties favoured it. Practically, all of them were of the opinion that India, with its large size, vast population and rich natural resources had no other viable economic option than to meet the growing needs of the country through a heavy involvement of the state. Even leaders in the private industrial sector considered that India's industrialisation would have to take place through a concerted effort by the government and the industry, in the face of what was perceived in Indian circles as a hostile international environment. The broad consensus on the subject was an optimisation of a fairly well-established economic thinking which had been formulated even before the independence of the country. As early as 1938 the National Planning Committee of the Indian National Congress, composed of hard-headed business, labour and left wing leaders had jointly envisaged such a strategy. Similarly the 1944 National Plan (known as the Bombay plan), prepared by the Indian businessmen, stressed the central role the State would play in the process of industrialisation; for in their view "an enlargement of the positive as well as the preventive functions of the State is essential to any large scale planning."[12]

In sum, India thus had clearly opted for an economic strategy which was inward looking, and which would economically insulate it from adverse global ramifications and unavoidable global pressures.

Economic nationalism, thus, was fundamental to India in the early years.

Nonetheless, paradoxical as it may seem, it must be pointed out that the outside world was not perceived as unimportant for Indian growth. While stressing the vital importance of the domestic internal growth through the instrumentality of the State, with trade and private capital inflows as minimal, International economic assistance was not rejected. If anything it was welcomed and even encouraged. In fact, Indian diplomacy was actively deployed for the obtainment of official international economic assistance. For the harsh reality and concatenation of circumstances were such that it could not ignore the benefits that would accrue from some interaction with the international economic system. Even the very success of its import substitution policy were heavily contingent on an opening to the outside world.

There was, at the time of independence, a great paucity of food and primary commodities in the country. India urgently needed them to feed its population and to furnish its industries. Already at the end of World War II the situation was serious. The system of rationing (introduced during the war) had to be continued and even extended. As many as 171 million people had to be covered by an elaborate scheme of rationing in 1947. In fact, so serious was the situation that the Commodity Prices Board, appointed in that year to review the overall situation, had come to the conclusion that the paucity of consumer goods was even more acute than during the war. The situation was rendered even more serious with the partition of the subcontinent since the bulk of food and raw materials were produced in areas that had become part of Pakistan.

At considerable cost to its limited foreign exchange reserves, food had to be imported.

Also India needed a wide array of machinery, equipment, technical assistance and so on for the development of its self-reliant economy. It could obtain this only from the outside. So the very goal of

Table
India's Food Grain Imports 1947-57 (in million rupees)

Year	*Quantity(000 tons)*	*Cost*
1947	2, 334	939.9
1948	2,841	1,297.2
1949	3,706	1.446.0
1950	2,125	806.0
1951	4,725	2160.0

Source : B.T. Ranadive, *The Crisis of the Indian Economy,* Bombay: Peoples Publishing House, 1954, (p. 119).

establishing an independent and autonomous economy required the implementation of an extensive policy of importation. Capital too was needed, if India wished to meet its ambitious goal of accelerated development. "Finance from abroad, and that too on a substantial scale," declared the Indian Finance Minister in early 1951, had to be forthcoming if the problem "of raising living standards has to be tackled adequately."[13]

The importance of seeking such assistance became all the more evident in the early sixties, since India was left with little sterling balances to draw upon, and since its already limited capacity to export had become even more constricted due to the rapidly developing domestic demand. "Foreign capital," declared the Indian Planning Commission, "is now indispensable to assure India's rapid growth."[14]

Thus, during the first three decades of economic development, Indian diplomacy was mobilised for the task of seeking official international assistance since private capital inflows was not what India wanted.

Soon after its independence, it was unavoidably faced with a dilemma. While on the one hand, it had opted for the development of a solid and autonomous economic base of its own, it had, on the other hand, realised that this was not possible without the import of primary goods and capital. One was linked with the other. But, what was even more problematic was that it did not have the financial capacity to pay for imports. Foreign reserves had indeed dried up. And items for exports were either severely limited or were, from the qualitative angle, either un-exportable or were already channelled into the rapidly growing domestic market. The Indian businessmen had in effect found a niche in the protective Indian market, and were really not interested in venturing out into the highly competitive outside market where the chances of their economic survival were minimal.

Under the circumstances, India had very few options. In fact, hardly any, except for actively striving to obtain official external assistance on favourable terms—terms that would be concessionary, and terms under which repayments would be effectuated as late as possible without excessively straining its economic structures.

In this connection India's announced foreign policy proved handy in surmounting this hurdle. Its politics of active nonalignment, compounded with the benign image it had already established internationally, buoyed hopes of viable interaction with the outside world. What was even more notable was that assistance stemmed from the two ideological blocs—undoubtedly a phenomenal feat that no developing country was able to realise with the same degree of success as India.

Though the politics of nonalignment was primarily a political choice—and had nothing to do with the hindsight economic interpretation that is now being advanced—the Indian leaders soon realised that they could reap considerable economic advantage of what was, at the time, a non-conformist foreign policy, They soon realised that some of the basic economic problems that India was faced with could probably be resolved through a well-designed diplomatic strategy. A special organisation of high level diplomats was, therefore, set up whose main task, in the words of its head, B.K. Nehru, was to induce "the developed world to part with its money."[15] In this context, a diplomatic strategy was designed towards the World Bank and the United States. The Polish economist, Kalecki, was even more explicit: the purpose of nonaligned aid strategy, in his view, was to create a situation under which "each bloc gives financial aid competing with each other."[16]

In fact, the aid was freely given by the Soviet and the Western world—often more than India had hoped for.

The nature of aid too was useful. It dovetailed with India's own economic strategy of development. For one thing, it was concessionary in the sense that long –terms loans, with lengthy grace periods were given by governments and multilateral organisations; for another, the aid was complementary in the sense that the nature of aid, emanating from the bipolar camp served India's purpose of simultaneously building an heavy industrial, agricultural and infrastructural bases, all perceived as vital in the process of modernisation.

Soviet Aid

Soviet aid was essentially industrial in content the principal objective of which was to establish a heavy industrial base—a base in which the Soviets had apparently acquired considerable experience after the Bolshevik Revolution. Much of India's negotiatory diplomacy was, therefore, geared to the task of identifying the industrial sectors in which the Soviets excelled, and which India could easily incorporate in its economic plans.

The list of industries finally established were wide-ranging. They included heavy metallurgical and mining machinery, oil exploration and production, steel mills, heavy electrical projects, petroleum refining, and pharmaceutical and surgical instruments. Its crucialness to the Indian economy can be gauged from the fact that almost one-third of India's steel and aluminium, more than 8o per cent of its metallurgical equipment and nearly half of its power and mining equipment was produced by Soviet aid. Many Indian scholars considered that the Soviet Union was "the most important source of external assistance to India,"[17] and that it contributed in placing India "among the top industrial nations."[18]

Though such an optimistic view was not shared by all observers[19] since the total Soviet assistance received between 1951-52 to 1983-84 was far less than what emanated from the west, there is nonetheless a large Indian consensus that Soviet assistance did provide "the important pillars" of a "fast expanding industrial structure."[20]

TABLE 2
Soviet and Western Bilateral Assistance 1951-52 to 1983-84(Rs Billion)

Aid	*Amount*
Bilateral Western Assistance	183,92.592
Soviet Assistance	1, 236. 65

Source: Government of India, *External Assistance* 1983-84 (New Delhi: Ministry of Finance, 1985).

Whatever judgement one might eventually make of the Indian model of economic development, as it was originally conceived, or of the nature of Soviet assistance, there does not appear to be any doubt that the "important pillars" of Indian economy, built by Soviet assistance, gave the country what the Indian leaders really wanted: a heavy industrial base that would help it to eventually become an economic power in the international system. That this, to some extent, is the case is evident in the 21st century when India is now generally perceived as one of powerful developing nations with great potential.

Would this current evaluation of India's growing economic power—of which practically everyone is talking about at the turn of this century— have had any real credibility without India's determination to go the industrial way.

Interestingly China had also undertaken a similar economic, though not a political path, during the Maoist phase of the Chinese revolution—a path of industrialisation. And, one wonders if the international consensual perception today regarding China's current economic leap would have been possible without the preceding heavy industrialisation undertaken during the Maoist phase.

Is it not striking that the two countries (India and China), which are today generally perceived as the real vanguard of economic growth in the 21st century, would have acquired such a gigantic status without the initial phase of industrialisation.

Russia on the other had, which was in fact the pioneer of heavy industrialisation during the Soviet phase, is the one which failed since it is today a country full of economic problems. The attribution of this failure was not so much due to the economic options it had taken, as it was due to distorted and horrendous political policies—brutal and thoughtless—followed during the Stalinist period.

While all this fleeting comparative analysis—for they are fleeting—may or may not have any great validity a serious in-depth analysis would be useful.

The bias for building a heavy industrial base also has something to do with the giantism of India. For it was hardly conceivable (at least at the time) that a gigantic country of India's size and market could ever have envisaged producing what the world needed rather than what India needed. The Indian scale, as pointed out by one writer, "does indeed support the hypothesis that giant economies march to a significantly different drummer."[21] The same probably may be the case in regard to China.

Thus, whatever judgement one may pass, or whatever evaluation one may make of Soviet assistance, it is undeniable, from this point of time, when other economic options have been taken, that India has indeed acquired an important industrial base which is making it possible for the country to establish an impressive growth rate that gives it a large potentiality regarding the future of Indian economy.

Similarly, one could also argue that the industrial base established in China, during the Maoist period, may have stood in good stead for China to make the great economic leap in post-Maoist China.

While India had largely a regulated economy within a democratic framework during the first phase, China had a regulated economy under a totalitarian framework. It could, therefore, be argued that it was probably the regulated phase of the two economies that gave them a solid industrial base, the ramifications of which are discernible today with clear signs of fast growth rates.

Western Aid

Western concessionary aid, on the other hand, was essentially, though not completely, agricultural and infrastructural. Paradoxically, most of it—if not all—were directed to the public sector thus contributing "to the socialisation of the Indian economy."[22] The measure of interest the Western world showed in India, including its non-aligned posture, can be discerned from the quantum of countries that disbursed aid. Almost all the members of the Organisation for Economic Cooperation and Development (OECD) helped India through Aid India Consortium. They included bilateral accords under which India received financial and/or technical assistance for the development of its infrastructure and/or the development of its agriculture. The United States was, by far the greatest contributor. Much of it, including the PL 480 programme, was focussed on India's urgent food needs, and on expanding its agricultural production.[23] In this context it is important to note that the role of private US Foundations was not negligible. For not only had they (invited by the Indian Government) extensively studied the different ways and means of expanding food production, but they had actually contributed to the meeting of these goals.[24] It was at the behest of the Ford Foundation that the Indian Government imported high-yielding wheat, maize and rice varieties that had been developed in centres in Mexico and the Philippines, which changed the very structure of Indian agriculture leading to the so-called green revolution, making India self-sufficient.[25]

Parallel to bilateral assistance from OECD countries, multilateral agencies became a "major channel of concessionary assistance to low income developing countries."[26]

These organisations provided the largest aid to India, much more than received by any other country; in fact much more than what was received by the top ten countries combined together in the sixties and the seventies.

According to some estimates India received as much as 20 billion dollars between 1951-89, most of which was directed at the public sector.[27] Indeed, India had developed very privileged relations with the World Bank. So much so that semi-official historians of the Bank have suggested that "no country has been studied—" and that no country has influenced the Bank's conception of the development process as India.[28]

TABLE 3
The International Development Association's Ten Largest Borrowers 1961-81

Country (*Dollars millions*)	*IDA's commitments*
India	9,556.2
Bangladesh	1,755.2
Pakistan	1,446.9
Egypt	981.2
Indonesia	931.8
Tanzania	631.8
Sudan	595.5
Sri Lanka	536.6
Kenya	458.3
Ethiopia	443.1

Source: World Bank. IDA in Restrospect: The First Two Decades of International Development Association, Oxford: Oxford University Press, 1982, p.11.

India was also a major recipient of International Monetary Fund (IMF) loans. Since its independence, it has been a beneficiary of one or another IMF programmes Several times in the seventies it received short term loans for balance of payments support. Its biggest borrowing—$ 5.8 billion— during the first phase, was negotiated in 1980 under the Fund's "Extended Facility Fund."

What was the effect of all this on India? Did it achieve the modernisation it strove for? Did it really benefit from international assistance ? And was it able to keep its hold intact on the economy while receiving assistance.

Thirty years of domestic effort did have a positive effect on the economy. For one thing, India did succeed in establishing a heavy industrial base. For another, it became self-sufficient in agriculture. For still another, it acquired a large pool of skilled manpower in a wide array of sectors—a triple achievement that hardly any other country had attained in the developing world.

Though, it is difficult to separate the external economic components from India's own domestic efforts, it has been argued that foreign aid "played an important role in permitting public and corporate to take place well ahead of the development of the household sector's propensity to save."[29]

It is important to note that all these significant achievements in the economic sector were made when the Indian economy was inward looking with import substitution as the main instrument with minimal foreign trade, with hardly any foreign capital, and with the Indian economy rapidly becoming "the most regulated economy in the non-communist world."[30]

Undoubtedly. this was a unique model of development since what the world had experienced was either a Western unimpeded movement of capital with free trade, or Soviet autarkical development within the frontiers of the nation. With such a strategy, India was able to expand right up to the seventies without facing any major disequilibrium in its international economic relations. Its overall deficit was not excessive since it did not exceed 600 million dollar mark and since foreign borrowing averaged only seven per cent of India's GDP, which was about one-third of the ratio for all developing countries taken together. Furthermore, India relied on debt on concessional terms with debt to official creditors constituting roughly 95 per cent of the gross external liabilities in 1970. The proportion of public debt at variable interest rate was as low as 0.4 even as late as 1978. The average maturity period on loan commitments to official creditors was 44.8 years (with 9.3 years as grace period) in 1978.

Emergence of Problems

But all this changed by the end of the seventies. The economy began to sputter. Problems emerged, both internally and externally, seriously threatening the ongoing Indian strategy of development.

Domestically, it became evident, after almost thirty years of planning, that the performance of the Indian industry, in terms of growth and employment generation, was disappointing. Though India had established an industrial base it was not self-sustaining. The original strategy of focussing on capital goods sector, on the ground that it would become self-sustaining, did not materialise. The gap between the actual and targeted rates of industrial growth began to widen.

TABLE 4

Targeted and Actual Rates of Growth (per cent per annum)

Plan Period	*Target*	*Actual*
First Plan (1951-56)	—	7.3
Second Plan (1956-61)	8.3	6.6
Third Plan (1961-66)	11.1	9.0
Fourth Plan (1969-74)	8 to 10	4.7
Fifth Plan (1974-79)	7.0	5.9

Source: India: A Reference Annual, New Delhi: Publications Division, Government of India 1974.

The infrastructure sectors also began to stagnate due to under-investment. Investments in the railways actually declined in seven out of the ten years following 1965-66. This was a major setback since investments in the railways, along with electricity and mining, accounted for 36 per cent of the total public investment. The share declined to less than 29 per cent in the seventies. Besides, the infrastructural constraints, arising out of the slowdown in public investments, industrial growth was also inhibited which sought to serve highly dispersive objectives while relying on excessive regulations and controls.

The agricultural sector too began to stagnate. The growth rate did not accelerate. At best, it remained constant. Besides, it was neutralised by the lack of any success in population control. After having declined from 40 to 30 per 1,000, the birth rate began to stagnate at 33 per 1,000. The growth of per capita income was only about 0.5 per cent per annum.[31]

The skilled manpower that India had created, after decades of considerable effort in education, began to migrate to other countries for better jobs and for better lives. India was no more in a position to absorb the skills it had generated. Immigration to the United States, for example, took a quantum leap in the early seventies. In 1969 the figure was 5,963. In 1970 it doubled, and by 1977 it had more than trebled.

Problems were even more insurmountable in the external sector. The trade deficit increased considerably, leaping to 2,239 million dollars in 1978-79, and finally capping at 7,546 million dollars in 1984-85. Apart from the fact that there appears to exist a rampant trend of trade deficits among developing countries as a whole, since they tend to import more than they can export, the growing gap in the case of India was also widened due to two specific reasons.

The first was the two oil shocks that India faced in seventies. The one in 1973-74 increased the deficit in the current account from 0.8 per cent of the GDP to 1.8 per cent in 1974-75. During the second oil shock, the import costs increased from 1,619 million dollars in 1978-79 to 3,122 million in 1979-80, and soared to 5,138 million in 1981-82.[32]

The second contributing factor to the widening gap in trade deficit was the overseas buying spree in the defence sector. Though the trend was already visible in the sixties it was accentuated in the eighties.

On the other hand, concessional capital inflows did not make any significant progress. Though the growth continued to increase, but only decliningly. From 750 million dollars in 1971-72 it increased to 1,128 million in 1974-75 and finally stagnated around 1,272 million dollars in 1981-82.[33]

Private investments were even slower in coming. The restriction, imposed by the highly rigid Free Exchange Regulations (FERA) made it extremely difficult for investments to enter. The growth in the number of foreign collaborations increased from only 20 in 1977 to 74 in 1980—undoubtedly a slow process.

By the late seventies, India, thus, was facing a different ball-game. The domestic economy was stagnating. The original expectations of India of becoming self-sustaining did not materialise. And externally a slew of unexpected developments, compounded with defence and the growing deficit in the balance of payments had increased the Indian level of dependence on the international economic system. The adverse ramifications of the growing trend towards the ongoing globalisation was catching up with India. No more could the Indians bask in the illusory glory of remaining largely detached from the international economic system.

THE SECOND PHASE

Growing Marketisation and Globalisation

The aggravation of India's economic problems did have some effect on the decision makers. Something had gone wrong. The original optimistic projections regarding the future of Indian economy had not materialised.

In the face of the declining situation, all the Indian Prime Ministers, from Indira Gandhi to Chandra Shekhar (1980-90), adopted a string of ad hoc measures to contain the deteriorating situation. Each of them took some incremental action and adopted some measures to this effect.

But, all these reforms, though meritorious, were taken within the ideological framework of keeping India as autarkical as possible in which the State continued to remain the primordial and decisive actor. Clearly, they were inadequate for a rapidly spreading disease. They were simply not enough to extricate the economic system from its lethargic state. What was needed was a radical treatment.

After some initial hesitation and ambivalence, dictated by political factors, the reform process was unfolded by the Narasimha Rao Government in the early nineties. In the aftermath of another hike in oil prices, and dramatic evaporation of foreign reserves, his government decided to make a real qualitative liberalisation and globalisation. Though it had its slow, cautious, and pragmatic beginnings in 1991, the whole process has continued since then more or less uninterruptedly to this day. Interestingly, no successive government attempted to turnaround the economy, or to backslide or to reconsider the new path chosen. A new and a secular process had indeed set in with no major challenges from any mainstream political groupings.

Here is an interesting example of the Indian economy making a major economic turnaround, leading the system towards an another direction. While the democratic system, known for its potteringness, does have the capacity of mutating whenever it is becomes necessary. Besides, it gives the whole changing process greater solidity and greater legitimacy since the level of interaction among thinkers and leaders is far greater before the actual initiative is taken; whereas in most other systems decisions tend to be thoughtlessly speedy with gregarious ramifications.

During the two decades that have elapsed since the inauguration of economic reforms, successive governments, notwithstanding their different political orientations, have uninterruptedly continued the process of deregulating the economy, by doing away with slowing-moving, bureaucratically controlled, industrial licences, by removing all registration formalities, by making the currency convertible in all account transactions, by clearing the way for foreign investments in most industrial sectors, including infrastructure and energy, and by opening the doors for an accelerated movements of imports and exports.[34]

In many ways the new path chosen was almost a revolution. For it was, in effect, taking India firmly away from a highly regulated and highly insular economy to a more open one. It required a new mindset and completely a new approach. The Minister of State for Commerce in 1992 made it clear to this effect. Speaking to potential foreign investors he assured them that India had, in effect, "ushered in an irreversible revolution to deregulate and liberalise its economy and trade."[35]

But, this change was less, problematic and less painful than in most Marxian operated economies. For one thing, India had a mixed economy with already existing fair-sized private sector, with a third largest functioning stock market; and a sizable segment of the Indian elite well—equipped with managerial gifts. For another, notwithstanding Nehruvian rhetoric in favour of socialism, most of the Indian leadership was well-versed with the techniques of making a market economy function efficaciously. For still another, India had a number of windows open to the outside world, including a forceful diplomacy that had made it possible for the country to have a vast network of amiable relations with most of the actors of the world. Besides, the entire elite and the decision makers were well conversant with the English language—a language that had achieved an international status—not to speak of the fact that the country's political system was helpfully democratic, making it easier to transit to marketisation and globalisation.

Contrastingly the communist countries, economically insulated from the developed western world, and distrustful of the intentions of the capitalist countries, had much greater difficulties of making a smooth transition to more open economies. Neither their ideological orientation nor the rigidity of their system permitted them to do so. Besides, moving away from a closed totalitarian political system—incompatible as it was to marketisation and globalisation—made things even more problematic to effectuate the changeover.

The Russian transition is indeed very difficult and is facing a whole series of egregious internal and external problems. Though, China, on the other hand, has come a long way from its original State controlled and State dominated system, a closer look at the transitional process shows the myriad difficulties it is faced with.

The Indian transition, thus, is incomparably less difficult and less painful than those of the communist countries.

The Indian Transition

What led the Indian decision makers to transmute the economy. How come that Narasimha Rao was able to do so where others had feared to tread. Why did he not—like his predecessors—introduce incremental and ad hoc changes to paper over the difficulties, while maintaining the original character of the economy. After all he was no more liberal and no more pragmatic than the previous Prime Ministers; for he had spent much of his political career—like his predecessors—talking of the socialist pattern of society, Besides, he was known to be an indecisive person who had great difficulties of taking any decision—least of all anything that would change India's political or economic road map.

The real catalyst was the rapid deterioration of India's external economic difficulties. Though the country had always lived with an adverse balance of payments, it had escalated exponentially; and by the time Rao took office in 1991, India's financial house was on the verge of collapsing. The economy was "running out of time."[36] In fact, it had come very close to defaulting on its $ 70 billion debt. To survive economically, and to maintain India's credibility, there was hardly anything else it could do but to turn to the IMF and the World Bank (WB) for loans to reverse the trend. For this, India had to pay a price—high price to obtain their imprimatur. "Every money lender," argued rightly Bahaduri and Nayyar "has his rates," and the IMF and the WB had theirs.[37]

But it was not only the Indian external economic environments that were teetering. Domestically the socio-economic conditions were also transmuting. By the 80s, it had become more than evident that the overall performance of the mixed Indian economy was hardly impressive. While it had certainly helped the country to build an array of heavy industries thereby changing its very industrial landscape, it did not visibly improve the lives of people. For most of the population, the

Nehruvian economic system had, in fact, deteriorated their lives, and destroyed their illusion of the viability of the economic system. What the state-centred economy had done was to project on to the scene an overwhelmingly powerful state which worked "on behalf of itself—the politicians, bureaucrats and the interests that directly support them."[38]

However, if the lives of the people had not palpably improved, the expanded state-centred system had nonetheless injected some transformation among the elitist group. It was slow and subtle process that had already begun years before, but had surfaced in the 90s. It was one of those sociological phenomena that do not suddenly emerge from one day to the other, but slowly matures itself in the fullness of time. The intellectual elite, generated by the British, and which had given the ideological direction to the country, had begun to efface. The broad socialist direction, it had given to the intellectual life of the country had failed; and the intellectual hold it had exercised on the decisional process began to show signs of slackening. What was perhaps worse, and even more tragic, was that no real attempt was made to re- adapt and re-adjust the original Indian elitist ideas to the changing situation. They were simply jettisoned, For, with the downfall of communism many of them began to show signs of bending themselves to the new intellectual winds of liberalism, market economy globalisation, etc. The growing irrelevance of their original ideas, and their own rapid conversion had discredited them. What was even worse was their insularity from changing India. The traditional elite neither fitted into the new grass-roots based new rural political elite that was being thrown up in the regions, nor could they relate themselves to the new emerging elite whose broad framework of thinking was neither macro nor abstract, but was oriented towards seeking ways and means of producing more and making more money. The new basic criteria of success was "a proven ability of getting things done"[39]

Another significant social development was the incrimination of the non-intellectual consumer-oriented middle class. Though such a group, of course, had existed, even during the time of the British, the growth of the state centred economy had already generated a respectable quantum increase during the first phase of India's modernisation. But, with the operationalisation of the reformist phase of the economy in the early nineties, India's middle class has finally taken wings reaching the 300 million mark. And according to the Mckinsey Global Institute (MGI) it is set to become the fifth largest consuming economy (behind US, Japan, China and the United Kingdom) in the next two decades.[40] The MGI report entitled "The Birth of Gold: The Rise of India's Consumer Market" "India's economic growth," it declares, "has accelerated significantly over the past two decades and so too has the spending power of its citizen... With rising income, household consumption has soared and a new middle class has emerged. And as the income growth rolls across Indian society, a huge shift is under way from spending on necessities such as food and clothing to household appliances and restaurants."[41] The report predicts that growth and consumption will spread beyond the top-tier cities, and has estimated that "almost two-thirds of India's middle class opportunities will be outside" the top-tier urban areas.[42]

Interestingly, this trend is already visible in some sectors. From December 2007 to December 2008 the number of rural mobile phone subscribers has increased from 60.4 million to 90.3 million. And according to Ernst and Young and Confederation of Indian Industries that out of next 250 million users, 100 million or 40 per cent will be from rural India.[43]

However, notwithstanding this new trend, the 300 million middle class Indians can hardly be compared to the Western Middle Class. While its consuming capacity is not negligent the products for them "have to be specially designed so that they are affordable"[44]

It is thus the emergence of the two new social groups (intellectuals and the consumer-oriented middle class) who are pushing India more and more towards an open, globalised and market economy.

The Evolution of Change

The remarkable quality of this new process of change was pragmatism, consentaneity and continuity. The move away from a state controlled autarchic economy to a more open and competitive was handled prudently. When the process of change was inaugurated in 1991 the strategy, according to Manmohan Singh the then Finance Minister was "to bring about a macro economic stability on the shortest possible period and then to launch a wide ranging programme of structural reforms to increase the dynamism of our industrial economy, exports and financial system."[45]

While the macro economic stability was introduced rapidly, the structural reforms were handled prudently and slowly. Coalition politics had overtaken the country, creating major difficulties of governance and rapid decision making; for there were indeed periods when the game of musical chairs and left wing pressures diverted the leadership's attention from the task of continuing the reforms at an accelerated period.

Nonetheless, while the mainstream political parties converged on the question of reforms, they often disagreed or hesitated regarding the pace and dimension of structural reforms—coalition politics oblige.

In any event, what is remarkable is the element of continuity, for none of the successive governments made any attempt to take India back to autarkical policies. Notwithstanding, the extreme leftist opposition to this process the trend was indeed becoming secular. The 2009 general elections should make the process easier, since the leftist opposition has become marginal, and should now be unable to slowdown the process as it has done in previous years.

In sum, during the two decades that have elapsed since the inauguration of reforms, the successive governments have continued the process of deregulating the economy, by doing away with industrial licences, by removing all registration formalities, by making the currency convertible in all account transactions, etc.

While all this was certainly important it was really at the international level that there were growing signs of new Indian options to integrate the country into the global economy—signs that were nonetheless cautious and prudent since it was the first time that India was attempting to reach out to the world economically.

The first major ramification of the new external policy was the exponential increase in trade. The various measures taken did have some effect. The share of trade in GDP increased considerably. It went up from 10 per cent in 1970s to 13 per cent in the eighties, to 20 per cent in the nineties and to 33 per cent in 2006 thereby reaching the impressive figure of 1 per cent of global trade in 2006-2007 (Trade 5)

India's remarkable trade performance can be attributed to various measures taken by the successive governments. The first was clearly the discovery of new markets. Second was competitiveness enhanced by the continuous depreciation of the Rupee since 1992. Though it did appreciate in 2006, exports nonetheless continued to rise. The third was that import policies were continuously liberalised; though there were ups and downs, there was nonetheless a secular trend in Indian determination to open the market. But the most dramatic development was in April 1999 when the Indian Government—in anticipation of its commitment to the

TABLE 5

India's trade 1984—2007 (US million dollars)

Year	*Imports*	*Exports*	*Total*
1984-85	9,878	14,412	24,290
1987—88	12,089	17,156	29,245
1994 – 95	28,645	26,330	54,984
1997—98	38,807	32,441	71.248
1999-2000	47,212	37,599	84,811
2005—2006	660,409	456,418	1116, 817 (crore Rs.)
2006-2007	862,302	571,649	1433, 951 (crore Rs.)

Sources: International Monetary Fund & Confederation of Indian industries.

WTO to slowly abolish import licences by the year 2003. By 2008 all the restrictions were abolished with the exception only of 58 items.

It is this policy that has improved the availability of imported intermediate and capital goods, thus reducing the bottlenecks to potentially exportable industries. The third major decision was to extend and streamline an array of taxes and non-taxes incentives to export the profitability of export industries.

The strong growth of exports right up to 2006 was due to commodity and geographical diversification. Though the commodity diversification was in the manufactured goods sector, there has nonetheless been a significant rise in the export of petroleum products and capital goods thus becoming the third most important category in India's total exports after gems, jewellery and pharmaceutical goods. But the most significant boost that India received was in the global diversification of the market.[46] While efforts were deployed all over the world, the ones that became crucial were the European Union, Persian Gulf, Japan, Southeast Asia and China.

European Union

The most striking foreign trade development was with the European Union (EU). Having become conscious of the emergence of the EU, India began to take important steps to accelerate domestic adaptations to the establishment of single European market in 1993—a market that has indeed become dimensional, and with whom an important "partnership and development agreement" was concluded in November 1993, that provided market access to the "highest possible degree" to the two signatories.[47] The process of India-EU has become uninterruptedly continuous as a result of which a series of agreements and accords were concluded, including the institutionalisation of regular summit meetings the most recent of which took place on 29 September, 2008 in Marseilles, France.[48] Without going into all the details of India-EU interaction—for this is not the purpose of this exercise—suffice it to say that an agreement on "strategic partnership" was concluded, and that negotiations are under way for the conclusion of a Free Trade Agreement (FTA).

The importance of India- EU relations can be discerned from the fact (a) that EU has become India's largest trading partner accounting for 19 per cent of trade, and (b) that its total foreign trade reached 40 billion Euros in 2005 far beyond India's expectations, since Indian Prime Minister Atal Behari Vajpayee had expressed, at the India-EU Summit in Lisbon 2000, his hope that India-EU trade would increase from US$ 20 billion in 1999 to 30 billion by 2005 and to 40 billion by 2010.

Persian Gulf

The Arab Gulf Region (Saudi Arabia, Kuwait, United Arab Emirates, Qatar, Bahrain and Oman), established a regional grouping under the name of Gulf cooperation Council (GCC), is another growing market for trade. India's interest in the area is due to a number of factors, including historical, geopolitical and economic. But, the predominant one clearly is the massive size of its market, its richness in capital, and India's acute dependence for oil from the area—a very vital source of energy for Indian economic development.

India's volume of trade with GCC has increased four-fold between 2002 and 2007. It reached 28 billion by 2007 and is expected to exceed $40 billion by 2010 provided the Free Trade Agreement, under negotiations, is agreed upon by the two parties concerned. The GCC has emerged as the third largest trade partner for India, after EU and the US.

The scope of capturing the GCC market is seriously constricted by the fact that most of India's exports are in such non-manufactured items as meat, fish, vegetables, spices and tobacco—items in which demand is inelastic. On the other hand, the diversification of exportable items in the industrial Sector has proved problematic since the Gulf countries were principally interested in high-tech for which they have a bias for the western world. The entire industrial framework in the area is being built in western technology, Besides, the main outlet for hydrocarbon and petrochemicals is the West.

ASEAN

ASEAN, now composed of 10 countries (Brunei, Cambodia, Indonesia, Laos, Malaysia, Myanmar, the Philippines, Singapore, Thailand and Vietnam) has become an important focal point of Indian economic diplomacy after 1991. The political sign of this interest was Prime Minister, Narashima Rao's, visit to all the Southeast Asian countries, with the exception of Brunei.

Though attempts were made to forge some degree of economic interaction with all the members of ASEAN, Singapore and Malaysia, in the beginning were, singled out as India's major economic partners because of the traditional ties with the two of them, and because they had large segments of Indian residents who had emigrated and had firmly installed themselves there.

However, with the consolidation of ASEAN as a regional entity and its later expansion to the whole area, compounded with India's inclusion into full dialogue partnership with the organisation, a new impetus and a new dimension was given to Indo-ASEAN economic cooperation.[49]

In the sector of trade India has done exceptionally well "witnessing the fastest rate of growth compared to any other region."[50]

Indo-ASEAN trade is thus becoming buoyant. It grew by 13 per cent during April-September 2007 to $ 17.02 billion, as against 15.06 billion during 2006 (same period). ASEAN has become India's fourth largest partner after EU, US and China. India's trade has been growing at a compounded annual growth rate of 27 percent, and is projected to reach 48 billion in 2008-09. With the conclusion of the Free Trade Agreement, which is expected to eliminate tariffs on 80 per cent of the items, the trade so expected to surpass even 50 billion.[51]

China

However, notwithstanding political problems between the two countries, Sino-Indian bilateral trade is continuing to grow by leaps and bounds. The trade value, during the first half of 2008, had already reached the 29-billion mark. And the two countries have programmed to raise their bilateral trade to 60 billion by 2010—a target set by the Prime Ministers of the two countries in 2005.[52] Given the complementary nature of the two gigantic economies, trade potential is considerable; and if the two countries conclude free trade arrangement, that is under way, the trade between them should take even a greater leap in the years to come.

The key items of India's exports are ores, slag and ash, iron and steel, plastics, and organic and inorganic chemicals. They accounted for almost 81.4 per cent during 2004-05.[53] On the other hand India's imports from China present a more balanced picture with resources based and manufactured products. The key items imported in 2004-05 from China included electrical machinery and equipment, mineral fuels, organic chemicals and silk.

Though there are vast opportunities a notable factor in trade relations is the rising Indian trade deficit each year. The trade deficit with China rose from the level of 816 million in 2002-03 to 9.159 million in 2006-07.

Japan

Japan is another important trade partner on India's list of priorities. Already before the introduction of the politics of liberalisation there were some signs of upliftment of Indo-Japanese trade relations. Trade figures, for example, had shot from 1.909 million dollars in 1984-85 to 2,880 million in early 90s. But, it was really the Indian landmark decision to opt for the politics of liberalisation that catalysed a more significant trade interaction. While the rate of trade growth was rapid doubling since 2001, it is still small with Indian exports reaching the 4.1 billion mark in 2007, and the Indian imports reaching the 6.1 figure during the same year.[54] But this acceleration had one major impact: India developed a deficit in its balance of payments. Whereas the trade trend was favourable to India up to 1994, the reverse trend appeared in 1995 and continues to remain to this day. Though this can be partially explained by the important fact that Japan had a much greater tradition and experience in matters of trade with India, the main reason was India's urgent and imperative need to import sophisticated machinery in order to prepare itself for competition in the export sector. The heavy importation of Japanese material was expected to substantially contribute to the up-gradation of the quality and quantity of Indian products thus facilitating their access to the global market.

The structure of trade is also not favourable in so far as it is very "vertical" since India exports essentially three products—marine products, gems and jewellery and iron ore—and imports a large array of sophisticated items. Though some Japanese consider that "it is not befitting the stature of our two countries,"[55] It is important to note that the Japanese private sector presence is rising with as many as 840 Japanese companies having their branches in India.

SAARC

The South Asian Association For Regional Cooperation, consisting of eight members (India, Pakistan, Bangladesh, Nepal, Bhutan, Afghanistan, Sri Lanka and the Maldives) should be mentioned as potentially crucial after the liberalisation and the globalisation of India's economy. SAARC, with a population of 1.5 billion people is the largest regional grouping in the world. But, compared to the intra-bloc trade of other regions (NAFTA-37 per cent, EU-63 per cent and ASEAN—38 per cent) SAARC's intra-bloc trade is only 3 per cent. The slowness in trade interaction can be principally explained by the primacy of politics over economics in the region. Notwithstanding the institutional expansion of regional intra-trade facilitation accords like South Asian Preferential Trade Arrangement (1995) and the South Asian Free Trade Area (2006), political differences, mutual suspicion, fear of dimensional India, still dominate the behaviour of member states.

India has nonetheless taken a series of unilateral trade facilitation initiatives towards most of the member states, with the exception of Pakistan with whom political differences and mutual suspicion are optimal.

India's trade with SAARC however continues to grow, especially after the conclusion of SAFTA. From $ 4,816, 88 million in 2003-04 it rose to $ 5,205 in 2004-05 thus registering an increase of 8.07 per cent.[56]

CAPITAL INFLOWS

Along with the new politics of trade expansion, an active policy of seeking external assistance was also collaterally pursued to obtain a significant augmentation of capital inflows.

Multilateral Assistance

Multilateral assistance today accounts for 70 per cent of the total assistance to India. Since most of the multilateral loans, emanating from the World Bank and the Asian Development Bank, are at a market rate and are not concessional, alone account for 64 per cent of multilateral assistance (Table 6) While this has triggered a debate on the cost effectiveness of these loans and the

Table 6
Multilateral Assistance to India 1980—2007 (in million of US dollars)

Year	*Amount*
1990-91	2,210
1991-92	3,037
1992-93	1,859
1993-94	1,901
1994-95	1,434
1995-96	527
2004-05	13221 crores
2005-06	12466 crores
2006-07	13321 crores

Sources : World Bank and Government of India.

rationale of keeping these loans in India's portfolio, they continue to be important in India's development strategy. The grant component of both these portfolios is negligible.

Bilateral Aid

Bilateral aid, on the other hand, mostly comes in the way of grants, accounting for almost 80 per cent of total bilateral aid with loans accounting for merely 22 per cent.

The most important donor is Japan reaching the high figure of 241.41 billion yens in 2007 (loans, grants and technical assistance). The official development assistance is extended in the form of soft loans, grants, technical cooperation, etc. and is principally directed towards the construction and improvement of major infrastructural facilities like power, highways, bridges, water supply, etc.[57]

However, the Japanese politics of aid suffered a serious setback after the Indian nuclear blasts in May 1995; for Tokyo suspended all its grant assistance and froze its soft loans. But, this did not last long, since the Japanese reverted back to their policy of focusing on India, even more so than China.[58]

Commercial Borrowing

The third component of capital inflows was commercial borrowing from the international market. Up to the eighties, it was principally confined to the government, but in the nineties it became a generalised phenomenon with the private companies who were encouraged to borrow selectively for approved projects. The government inaugurated broad guidelines that the companies had to follow to obtain the necessary financial resources from outside of India. The guidelines—modified from time to time—indicated that the total amount of such borrowings must not exceed 8.5 billion dollars a year,[59] that they must be geared towards specified projects (infrastructure, shipping, exporters, etc.) with maturity specifications and with clear caps on the amount different economic sectors could borrow.[60]

Though the Government still closely monitors such capital inflows, due to the high debt ratio ($ 15 billion in 1996-97), commercial borrowings have become an ongoing process in which an increasing number of companies are becoming heavily involved; they are indeed in dire need of foreign exchange to continue their imports which cannot be met completely by exports.

Foreign Investments

Foreign investments are the fourth component of capital inflows. Originally, this channel was "viewed for the transfer of technology."[61] But, with the decline in the availability of concessional financing in the eighties,, and with the debt creating disadvantage of commercial borrowing for a government already in debt, greater emphasis shifted to foreign equity investments.

Under the new process of liberalisation, the Government has, therefore, taken a series of steps to remove procedural and economic hurdles in the way of investments—hurdles that had kept the international multinationals out of India. This was not a one shot affair, but an ongoing process of liberalisation that beckoned the multinationals to come to India. Profits, for example were allowed free convertibility and repatriation; taxations were considerably reduced on stocks owned by foreign companies (10 per cent) in comparison to their Indian counterparts (46 per cent); prior approval of the government was no more required

Table 7
Foreign Direct Investments (million dollars)

Year	*Amount*
1991-92	150
1992-93	344
1993-94	620
1994-95	1,314
1995-96	2, 133
2001-02	8,200
2003-04	21,400
2005-06	29,800
2007-08	63,800

Sources: Government of India, World Bank, International Monetary Fund.

for a wide segments of industries; and in sectors where such approval was needed, the Foreign Investment Promotion Board took rapid decisions. Finally, to take just one more example, foreign investors were no more restricted to their equity participation in joint ventures with Indian companies; they could have majority share, and they could establish 100 per cent subsidiaries when joint venture existed. The influx of direct and portfolio investments has thus increasingly become an integral part of the Indian landscape (Table 7)

Liberalisation of regulations with respect to foreign institutions, of course, is not an adequate condition for attracting inflows, but is obviously a necessary precondition for the process to be activated.

It was only after 2003 that the process of capital inflows really surged reaching the high figure of 63.8 billion dollars.

The major ramification of this surge was bank credits that grew at a scorching pace from 2005 at a more than double the rate of the normal gross domestic product. So much so that the bank credits reached 60 per cent of the GDP by the end of March 2008.

The financial liberalisation of the economic reforms has resulted in the credit dependence of the Indian economy, so much so that the growth in credit outperformed the growth in bank deposits resulting in the increase in credit deposit ratio from 55.9 per cent in March 2004-05 to 72.5 per cent in March 2008.

This increase was accompanied by a corresponding drop in investment-deposit ratio from 51.7 percent to 36.2 percent during the same period.

In sum, the banks were shifting away from their earlier preference to invest in government security to retail loans that rose from 27.2 per cent in March 2002 to 76 per cent at the end of March 2008. The most important item was the housing loans of "sub-prime" variety. According to some estimates by November 2007 there was in the vicinity of 400 billion rupees of credit that was of sub-prime quality.

This process is very much analogous to the US system. And signs are already surfacing that retail loans are defaulting, and that the growing exodus of foreign capital has created serious problems for Indian economy.[62]

Non-Resident Indians investments (NRIs)

The fifth form of capital inflows is NRI investments. Of the different type of external investments, this is becoming by far the most important source of overseas Indian investment. The rate of growth is striking, and is becoming the largest form of capital inflow.

The Indian Government, under the new liberalisation policy, has taken a number of initiatives to attract non-resident Indians to invest their savings, which, according to the Indian Finance Ministry, have reached more than 20 billion Dollars.

To encourage the new politics, the government has introduced the "PIO card Scheme" under which persons of Indian origin (fourth generation) are issued a card that entitles them to visit India without a visa, that frees them from having to register with the India authorities, and that allows them to acquire a series of rights similar to Indian nationals residing in India.[63] One of the crucial sectors to which NRI investments have been targeted is real estate—a sector that has the potential to touch USD $ 90 billion within the next five years. While, the regulations still do not permit NRIs to acquire agricultural land, plantations and farm houses, the urban property sector is open to them—a sector which has out-performed the other investment options. The NRIs can acquire residential immovable property (housing, commercial, retail shopping) and can repatriate their incomes to the countries of residence.[64]

Indian investments abroad

Another growing dimension is the new process of Indian investments abroad. Traditionally, capital moved from developed to developing countries—a movement that was generally perceived in the developing countries as a form of colonial exploitation. The reverse too is happening now. With a high growth rate, and easy access to foreign currencies, India, under liberalisation, has become an important exporter of capital. According to the data released by the Reserve Bank of India (RBI) the total direct investment has reached $ 46, 194, 35 million as of March 2008.[65]

While, originally 35 per cent of the FDI was directed at Singapore, the Netherlands, followed by British Virgin Islands, it has now become global. The importance of such investments, according to Grant Thornton, a global consultancy firm, can be discerned from the fact that, during the first 11 months of 2008 stood at 433 (merger and acquisition) deals with an announced value of $31.95 billion, thus exceeding the domestic ones in terms of value break.[66]

The whole objective of such a trend was to acquire new markets, maintain its own growth momentum, buy cutting-edge technology and leverage brand names for their brands.

In a bid to give further impetus to overseas investments, the RBI has introduced further liberalisation in their policies.

While the list has become too long, some of the most important ones are the acquisitions of UK-based Corus, by Tata Steel for about $ 8 billion, the German Firm, Repower Systems AG by Suzlon Energy Limited for $ 1.7 billion, and the takeover of Scotch whisky distilleries, WHYTE and Mackay by Vijay Mallya-led United Spirits for $ 1.11 billion.[67]

Ramifications of new policies

All these neo-liberal and globalisation policies, directed at the opening up of the economy, have had a beneficial effect on India's macro-economic performance. For the economy expanded at more than 5 per cent in the eighties, and even more in the nineties. After 2003 the average growth rate went up 8 ¾ percent making India one of the fastest-growing economies.

Besides, this process of growth has unleashed viable economic and social mobility: the middle class has grown to nearly 300 million people; more than 150 million have moved above the poverty line; mass communication has come of age with India becoming the second largest telecom user in the world after China and ahead of the US, with more than 400 million television viewers and with more than 100,000 video cassette shops across the country.

The demographic growth rate too has declined in the country from the annual rate of 2.2 percent in the seventies to 2.1 since the turn of the 21st century. And the literacy rate has gone up as much as 8 per cent, showing for the first time in the 21st century that more than half the population is able to read and write.

While much of all these benefits, of course, are urban-centred, the rural areas, albeit still living in grinding poverty and under-nourishment, are also witnessing some beneficial social effects of industrial and technological revolution. Literacy rate has increased, health hazards have been partially contained, and the level of rising expectations have become more rampant. One of the recent and most palpable development is the inundation of mobile phones into the rural areas. From December 2007 to December 2008 rural mobile phone subscribers has increased from 60.4 million to 90.3 million. Rural India is witnessing "a hunger of different kind, the urge to possess a mobile phone."[68] According to Ernst and Young and Confederation of Indian Industries report that, out of the next 250 million phone users, 100 million or 40 per cent will be in rural India thus changing "the dynamics of communication across to a majority of India's 600,000 villages."[69]

THE OTHER SIDE OF THE COIN

But, there is the other side of the coin. The politics of liberalisation has also spawned a vast array of problems and difficulties. Having increasingly become a part of the global economy, its economic fate is growingly linked with the fate of the rest of the world. It can no longer protect itself from the fluctuating economies of the international system, and can no more defy outright the pressures of powerful economies.

The gap between exports and imports have widened considerably. Though exports have continued to rise with India's determination to find additional markets, imports have been rising even faster—in fact, much faster than the original estimates. Though this is probably the unavoidable fate of most developing countries, which are striving to establish a broad and independent industrial base of their own, the seriousness of India's position can be attributed particularly to three factors: to the continuously escalating need of energy the demand for which continues to rise exponentially. Given India's ongoing determination to expand economically, this has clearly become a secular trend from which it can hardly retract; to the heavy importation of expensive and sophisticated military hardware that India is determined to buy abroad for which the demand is going to increase, even more, now that the South Asian political environment (Pakistan and Afghanistan) is deteriorating chaotically; and finally to the new expansive export strategy for which it needs a wide array of import items to renovate its export-oriented industries.

Since, the widening trade gap cannot be abridged by India's limited capacity to export, the only viable way out is to attract financial resources to fill in the growing deficit in its balance of payments.

This is what is being done. Since concessional aid was no more available in large quantities, India had to resort to commercial borrowings, to foreign direct investments, and to seek out expatriate capital from

NRIs, all of which have heavily increased India's external debt reaching the high figure of US$ 230.85 billion in December 2008.[70] But the situation is not perceived as alarming, since the India reserves have been growing and had in fact exceeded debt in 2004 for the first time. At the end of March 2005 India had the fifth largest stock of reserves in the world. Compared to other large debtor nations such as Brazil, Mexico, Turkey, etc., India's situation is much better since its debt ratio[71] to gross domestic product has come down from 21 percent to 17.4 in 2005.

While the situation is not difficult now, there is really no guarantee that India's external debt may not take a great leap in the future, given its exponential drive to import.

Whatever, may be the correct situation, one thing is certain India has substantially moved away from an inward economy. The policy of import substitution, carried out for almost thirty years, did not deliver the goods. Even if the vast size, resources, population, etc., have led the political leadership to the conclusion that India never could be a predominantly export-oriented and capital imported country, a consensus has indeed emerged that greater economic interaction and domestic adaptations have become necessary to meet the challenges of the outside world and of the 21st century.

The current economic meltdown the world is confronted with since 2008 had naturally also affected India. This is the price it had to pay for increasing liberalisation and globalisation of the economy. All sectors, linked to the global economy, had, therefore, been affected. The exports, which account for 15 per cent of the economy, have declined; foreign capital invested in India showed signs of exiting from the country: and the stock market, barometer of the state of Indian economy, had gone down by 40 per cent.

While all this was unavoidable, given global economic wrenching, it is nonetheless important to note that the effect on India was not as great as it was on the Western world, which was in the midst of a deep recession.

The explanation for this is traditional Indian economic prudence vis-à-vis the outside world. While realising the importance of liberalisation and globalisation for Indian economic growth, it was prudent enough not to immerse itself completely into the global economic system. It maintained some degree of distance and some degree of detachment, both of which have saved India from the vagaries of the international economic system. So what India was facing was an economic slowdown, and not a recession.

The Indian growth rate continued to remain high (5 per cent) even if it had lost its optimality, its rural market was booming, there were already some signs in 2009 that a number of foreign agencies had begun the process of flocking to India. In January 2009, it attracted $ 2.7 billion, up by 58.8 per cent from what it was a year ago, and remained a favourite destination for cross border investments.

The decision to liberalise and globalise the Indian economy was certainly a major landmark in contemporary Indian history. Who would have thought only two decades ago that the country would move in that direction? Who would have even imagined a few years ago that the entire spectrum of Nehruvian thinking and policies would be cast aside by his own followers? But then who would have predicted a few decades back that the whole Soviet empire would crumble, and all that it stood for and followed would be abandoned?

History is cast in such an unpredictable mould. Unexpected things do happen. Long periods of continuity, to which one gets used to, are often followed by short and tumultuous periods of change, only to be jettisoned for another long periods of continuity.

Only time will show if this process of economic change will deliver the goods. It is impossible to predict, with any degree of certainty, if India will be better off in this new century, or if the continuous globalisation of the Indian economy is going to mire India into greater uncertainty, confusion and discontent.

References

1. Shriman Narayan, *Towards a Socialist Economy,* New Delhi Indian National Congress, 1956, p. 10.
2. *Economic and Political Weekly,* 14 July 1964, p. 41.
3. M.K. Gandhi, *India of my Dreams,* Ahmedabad: Navjivan Publishing House, 1940, p. 24.
4. Jawaharlal Nehru, *Toward Freedom : An Autobiography of Jawaharlal Nehru*, New York: John Day, 1942, p. 401.
5. Michael Brecher, *Nehru a Political Biography,* Boston : Beacon Press, 1959 (abridged edition, p. 95.
6. Avadi Resolution (1955) of the Indian National Congress ; partial text in Shriman Narayan, op. cit., p. 1.

7. Terrance K. Hopkins, Immanuel Wallerstein and Associates, *World System: Theory and Methodology,* Beverly Hills: Sage Publications, 1982.
8. Jean Gottmann (ed), *Centre and Periphery : Spatial Variation in Politics,* London: Sage Publications, 1980.
9. Hopkins and Wallerstein, op.cit., p. 19.
10. Cited in Kalyan Banerji, "A more active role in India," *Business India 1978-88,* April 1988, p. 69.
11. Chalmers Johnson, "Political Institutions and Economic Performance in Japan, South Korea and Taiwan," in Frederic C. Deyo(ed), *The Political Economy of new Asian Industrialisation,* Ithaca: Cornel Univesity Press, 1987, p. 87.
12. C.D. Deshmukh, *Economic Development in India : 1946-1956 : A Personal Retrospective* :Asia Publishing House 1958, p. 70.
13. Ibid., p. 59.
14. Planning Commission, *Towards a Self.Reliant Economy : India's Third Plan 1961-66,* New Delhi: Publications Division, 1961, p. 135.
15. B.K. Nehru, "The way we looked for money abroad," in Vadilal Dagli (ed) *Two Decades of Indo-US relations,* Bombay: Vohra and Company, 1960, p. 21.
16. J. Osiatynski (ed), *Works of Michel Kalecki,* Oxford: Clarendon Press, 1993, p. 30.
17. Rama Shankar Singh, *Indo-Soviet Cooperation and India's Economic Development,* New Delhi: Deep and Dees Publications, 1989, p. 10.
18. R.K. Sharma, *The Economic of Soviet Assistance to India* New Delhi: Allied Publishers, 1981, p. 2.
19. P.J.S. Duncan, *Soviet Union and India,* London: Routledge (for the Royal Institute of International Affairs, 1989.
20. M.M. Dubey, Indo-Soviet Cooperation : Retrospect and Prospect, in V.V. Balabushshevich and Bimal Prasad (eds) *India and the Soviet Union: A Symposium,* New Delhi: Peoples Publishing House, 1969, p.92.

21. John K. Lewis, "Some consequences of Giantism : The case of India", *World Politics,* April 1991, pp. 388-389.
22. Shyam J. Kamath, *Foreign Aid and India : Financing the Levethian State,* Washington DC: Cato Institute Policy Analysis No. 170, 6 May 1992, p. 10.
23. D.N. Prasad, *Food for Peace : The Story of US Food Production in India,* Bombay: Asia publishing House, 1980.
24. Government of India, *Report on India's Food Crisis and steps to Meet It.,* Delhi: Ministry of Food and Agriculture, 1959.
25. For details, see ibid.
26. World Bank, IDA in Retrospect : *The First Two Decades of the International Development Association,* Oxford: Oxford University Press, 1982, p.V.
27. Shyam J. Kamath, op. cit.
28. Edward Mason and Robert E. Asher, *The World Bank since Bretton Woods,* Washington DC: Brookings Institution, 1973, p. 675.
29. Ibid., p. 675.
30. Robert W. Bradnock, *India's Foreign Policy since 1971,* London: Pinter, 1990, p. 47.
31. Isher Judge Alluwalia "Industrial Policy and Indian Performance" in India, in Robert E.B. Lucas & Gustav F. Papanek (eds), *The Indian Economy: Recent Developments and Future Prospects,* Boulder: Westview Press 1988.
32. Rangarajan, India's Foreign Borrowings in ibid.
33. Ibid.
34. For some details, see "A year of Reforms," *Business India,* July 6-19 1992; also see Frank Gibney Jr, "Riding the Tiger," *Newsweek,* August 31, 1992.
35. *Times of India*, 22 May 1992.
36. *India Today,* 31 December 1990, p. 21.

37. Amit Bahaduri and Deepak Nayyar, *The Intelligent Person's Guide to Liberalisation,* New Delhi: Penguin Books, 1996, p. 30.
38. Gurcharan Das "A million reformers now," *Business Daily.* p. 52.
39. Ibid. p. 52.
40. See Indrajit Basu "India's Middle class takes wings" *Asia Times.* June 1, 2007.
41. Cited in Ibid.
42. Ibid.
43. Devika Menon, "Trunk Calls to Ringstones," *Tehelka* 16 May 2009.
44. Darryl Monte, "The reality of the vast middle class," *The Sunday Times of India,* 3 October 1993.
45. "Interview with Manmohan Singh," *World Affairs*, January-March 1997, p. 22.
46. For details, see *Annual Report*, 2007-2008, New Delhi : Directorate General of Commercial Intelligence and Statistics, 2008.
47. Kamal Ghose, "India and Europe, 1992 : Possible effects on Imports," *Fortune India,* 16 December 1990.
48. For details, see "Eu-India Summit," *World Affairs,* Number 3, Autumn 2008.
49. Kripa Shridharan, *The Asean Region in India's Foreign Policy,* Aldershot: Dortmouth, 1996.
50. G.V.C. Naidu, *India and Asean,* Delhi Papers Institute of Defence Studies and Analyses, New Delhi: 1998, p. 42.
51. IBEF, India and ASEAN, *http://www.ibef.org/Indiaasean.aspx* 25 May 2009.
52. "India-China Trade scales new heights in first half," *The Hindu Business Line*, 9 September 2008.
53. *China Daily,* 26 May 2009.
54. Ministry of Foreign Affairs of Japan, "Japan-India Relations," *Internet*, 25 May 2009.

55. Speech of Hioshi Harabayashi, Japanese Ambassador to India ; for the text, see *Japan Economic Report,* Quarterly no 45, October-December 1998, p. 9.
56. G. Sirinivasan, "SAFTA : India should Lead by example," *Hindu Business Line,* 5 January 2006.
57. Sakutaro Tanino, "Indo-Japanese Economic ties," *Japan Economic Report,* January-March 1997.
58. Purnendra Jain, "Japan to Shift aid focus from China to India,"*Asia Times*, 11 March 2004.
59. Fordetails, see *Internet :http://www. altavistic. digital. com.*
60. Ibid.
61. India Investment Centre, *Opportunities, Technology and Collaboration,* New Delhi : 1986, p. 9.
62. For details, see March 2009 report of the official committee on financial sector assessment of the Reserve Bank. This was chaired by Rakesh Mohan, the deputy govorner of the bank; also see C.P. Chandrashekhar, "Economic Perspectives," *Front line,* 8 May 2009.
63. For details see *India News, 9th April 1999.*
64. Indian Ground. Com, "NRI investment in India," *http://www. Indianground.com/nri/nri_investments _in India,* O5.05.2009
65. IBEF, "Indian Investments Abroad," *htto://www.ibef.org,* 05.05.2009.
66. Ibid.
67. Ibid.
68. Devika Menon, "Trunk calls to Ringtones," *Tahelka,* 16 May 2009, p. 40.
69. Ibid, p. 40.
70. "India's External Debt rose to 230.85 bn dollars,"*http://blog. taragana. com/n/india's -external debt-rose-to 23085-bn-24030.* / 6/6/2009
71. "External debt not alarming," *http://www.hindu.com/biz/2005/07/.*

6

Society: Increasing Complexity

Nothing in India is identifiable, the mere asking of the question causes it to disappear or to merge in something else.

E.M. Forster 1924

The political and social evolution of India, since independence, has been eventful but not dramatic.

The firm institutionalisation and operationalisation of democracy had indeed generated unprecedented degree of political stability in the country. Barring only a brief period of political authoritarianism, imposed by Indira Gandhi, the country has continued to remain faithful to democratic institutions. They have developed and thrived during the last six decades, and have never been compromised or even questioned by any of the Indian governments.

This is one of the few issues on which there has always existed widespread consensuality within the country.

It is generally claimed that it is the prevalence of these democratic institutions that has given India the stability from which it has benefited during all these years.

While the 12 national elections that the country has been subjected to, since 1951, has given the vibrancy to the political system, the democratic institutions have evolved during all these years.

First of all, the Indian system is now subjected to coalition politics. Gone indeed are the days when one political party was large enough electorally to form a government on its own. While, there may be, of course, periods when a political party has acquired a comfortable representation in the Parliament, as was the case in 2009 national elections, the formation of one party government does not appear to be any more possible. Coalition politics has indeed become an indelible part of the Indian political system.

While for some observers this is a welcome development, as it mirrors the broad diversity of Indian politics, there are others who, on the other hand, tend to consider that coalition politics has injected some degree of instability and decisional indecisiveness into the whole political system.

One of the Prime Ministers, who was heavily mired in coalition politics, viewed such a situation as favourable to the political survival of the head of the government, since the tendency in coalition politics invariably was to refer the important issues to the political parties for decisions, thus causing considerable delay in the whole process.

The second dimensional mutation is the emergence of regionalism in Indian politics. Regions have become more assertive in national politics, and have acquired greater voice in national decision making, since, more often than not, many of them are a part of coalition governments.

On this point too national consensuality is absent. While, there are some who consider that regionalism has generated a high degree of inequality, since the ones which are large and powerful, would have greater weight in national politics than the ones which are smaller and less powerful.

Such an argumentation is countered by others who consider that the national emergence of regionalism forces the national leaders to take into account regional values and regional interests in the decisional process.

The third change was the slow but nonetheless visible gap between real political power and formal political office. The one who was holding office was not necessarily wielding real power. While coalition politics had generated this political phenomenon, the tendency became fixated with the emergence of a fleet of prime ministers mandated for brief periods; but even those like Narasimha Rao and Vajpayee, who were in office during two mandates, the centre of power was more diffused and more dispersed.

With Manmohan Singh political power and political office became clearly distinct. The only reason that Singh became Prime Minister was because he was appointed by Sonia Gandhi the real power centre. What is even more remarkable that Singh—perhaps the only one –who was not even elected, but was a member of the Rajya Sabha from Assam, the state of which he was not even a resident.

The combination of these three major developments have germinated major ramifications in Indian behaviour. The decisional process has slowed down, and the process of their actual implantation has decelerated considerably. While this is increasingly becoming a universal phenomenon among all political democracies, in India it is even more so given the country's political complexities and hinderous bureaucracy.

EMERGING SOCIAL GROUPS

The process of ongoing economic development, with the market-oriented economic reforms of the 90s of the last century has resulted in an economic upsurge in the country. While India still has a wide chunk of its population mired in poverty, living even below the Indian definition of poverty line, the two decades of vibrant economic development of nearly 8 percent per annum has mutated the overall economic picture of the country. India is now witnessing a growing middle class. It is there statistically expanding into a vibrant economic force. But the Indian middle class is hardly comparable to the one in the western world.

The one in the West has a mortgage on their residence, a car to drive, enough savings to go on vacations, to consume a balanced diet every day, and to send their children to schools and universities—not to speak of a wide array of gadgetry accessories they possess for their household.

While the upper middle class, composed of salaried professionals, whose work is self-directed, may be the one that is, on the whole, comparable to their counterparts in US and Europe.

Nonetheless the Indian economic vibrancy is pushing up a group of growing middle class. While. they can hardly be comparable to the ones in the West or even to the ones belonging to the upper Indian middle class, they are nonetheless showing signs of financial acquisition that goes beyond their basic needs. Though the economic differences between the two Indian groups is enormous, the one factor that is common is varying degrees of their capacities to consume—the rich naturally much more than the poorer segments.

With the ongoing high rate of growth the quantum of Indians who will enter the middle class is going to expand considerably. Using a broad income criterion of Rs. 35,000 per household the middle class that comprised 14 per cent of all households, and comprised 113 million people in 1993-93, has increased to almost 26 per cent of all households or almost 250 million in 1998-99. Given their continuous rate of growth the Indian middle class should expand to 583 million—some 41 per cent of the households—by 2025.[1] These households are expected to increase their income balloon to 51. 5 trillion rupees ($ 1.billion).—11 times the level of today and 58 per cent of Indian income.[2]

The Mckinsey Global Institute's report of May 2007, argued that India's much touted middle class "has finally taken wings."

India, thus, is unavoidably moving towards a middle class society—a society that will no more be more concerned with fulfilling its needs, but will be turning more and more towards its wants. And it one accepts Aristotle's idea that "good society is the one where the middle class outnumbers every one else," then India is moving in that direction.

But, according to all analyses of the middle class, it appears that it does not only represent consumerism—though this is important. For Aristotle a wide set of virtuous behavioural traits exist in the class hierarchy. They include willingness to rule without being over ambitious, to respect authority, good fellowship and reduced envy. These are essentially pertaining to individual behaviour.

Max Weber, on the other hand, deals with the community as a whole, pointing out the important role of democratic institutions. Weber was a key witness in the struggle of liberal middle class for Germany's external place in the world and its role in the internal democratic order. While the German sociologist failed in the face of Bismarck's authoritarianism, the vital importance of the middle class as a proponent of liberal democratic revolution became his basic thinking.

The Indian middle class is in the process of this transition. While it has focussed on consumerism, there are indeed signs that political ramifications are developing in favour of political aspects, including political stability and the strengthening democratic institutions Signs of such an interest became visible in the 2009 general elections where the middle class played a crucial role. With its further numerical expansion it is expected to become a basic pillar of democratic institutions in India.

The Dalits

If the growing middle class is a new phenomenon in Indian politics, the Dalit community of more than 160 million people is as old as history going back to more than a thousand years. Belonging to the lowest rung of the hierarchically based caste system, it has been the most exploited and the most humiliated group among the different groups living in India.

So much has been written about their past that it would be superfluous and indeed repetitive to delve lengthily about them in this treatise. Suffice it to say that since the onset of the 20th century, when the democratic process was injected into the Indian political system, there has been continuous and concerted attempts to ameliorate their status within the system.

There were the British who took a series of actions, including a separate electorate system, to assure their security and to ensure an appropriate system of representation. But, hardly any Indian leader favoured such a step, since it was conceived as a British strategy to divide the Indian population.

There was Gandhi who, calling them Harijans (children of god), insisted on their amelioration within the hinduist framework without any interference from the outside.

There was Dr. Ambedkar, educated in USA, UK and Germany—a Dalit himself—who devoted all his life to unite them and to uplift their status. As a constitutionalist, who devoted his time to draft the Indian constitution, he firmly believed in the importance of political democracy for their amelioration, but, at the same time, was sceptical of its efficaciousness, given the fact that democracy was a majoritarian rule that would place the high caste Hindus in positions of power. Ambedkar, therefore, devoted much of his time assuring constitutional rights to the Dalits so that they did not become victims of caste rule, Though he did not favour reservations, 17.5 per cent of the seats of the Parliament and the State Assemblies were reserved for the Dalits.

Since the independence of the country, there have been continuous and concerted efforts on the part of all successive governments, to improve their elective representation, and systematically passed laws to improve their status.

In the past two to three decades India has thus witnessed the real transfer of parliamentary power from the upper castes to the middle and backward castes; so much so that upper caste members of parliament fell below 50 per cent for the first time since 1977. And in the late eighties the percentage of dalit and other backward castes (OBC) representation doubled from 11 to 21 per cent in 1989, increasing to 25 percent by 1996.

This gradual transfer of legislative power was viewed by Prime Minister, V.P. Singh, as the "silent social revolution"[3] Even more important is the important fact that this has changed more dramatically at the state level.

Indeed, this was a "silent social revolution." For it had projected the Dalits on to the Indian electoral system—the ones who had been deprived of any power. The parliamentary and the State Legislative Assemblies were no more composed only of elitist groups, but now included members who were not educated, who were not familiar with the English language, and who were hardly omniscient with macro Indian politics. In sum the deprived had surfaced emitting on to the political scene a broad representation that mirrored real India.

But such a new spectacle also had its deficiencies. Since political democracy is a system of alliances, forged between political groups to reach governmental power, India now began to witness a new political spectacle of elected Dalit leaders seeking out other corresponding groups to establish governmental power. The immediate objective was no more to design an independent strategy to advance the interests of their constituents, but to seek power through alliances with other corresponding groups.

While this may be understandable in a political democracy—for all groups strive to reach power—the personal ambitions of established Dalit leaders resulted in the sad spectacle of governments being established that did not represent the interest of their constituents.

Consider the establishment of the Government in Bihar where one of the backward leaders made an alliance with Muslims that ruled the state for more than twenty years without doing any serious work. It was worst in UP where Mayawati, the Dalit chief minister, combined her caste strength of *Chamars* with the Brahmins, much to the resentment of the Dalit community.

The state government simply forgot the basic Dalit agenda of governance like land reforms, education, social health schemes or any real scheme for the poor. Besides, Mayawati became heavily involved in objectionable practices gaining the notorious distinction of having become the most corrupt leader in India. who has openly enriched herself. “Her anniversaries,” writes the French newspaper, *Le Monde,* “are sumptuous.” So much so that “in January 2008 she was served a birthday cake of 52 kilos to celebrate her 52 years.”[4] The governments, established by the Dalits and other marginalised groups, thus have generated serious crises in many of the Indians states. The mainstream political parties do not any more have the monopoly of such a distinction.

However, notwithstanding their legislative amelioration, almost 160 million Dalits still remain the prime source of discrimination within the country. Thousand years of intolerance, prejudice and unfairness has victimized their day-to-day lives. While their situation may have improved with the passage of time, and with their emergence as a legislative power, they are heavily targeted by high caste Hindus. Prime Minister Manmohan Singh likened their discrimination (27 December 2006) to the apartheid system in South Africa.

Human rights abuses of Dalits are indeed legion. A random sampling of the media headlines tells their tragic story. “A Dalit boy beaten to death for plucking flowers, “Dalit tortured by copy for three days,” “Dalit women paraded naked in Bihar, “Dalit women gang raped.[5]

Dalits are not allowed to drink from the same wells, disallowed to attend the same temples, prohibited to wear shoes in the presence of an upper caste Hindus, As late as 2009 a survey covering 5 districts in the South, having a population of 4,46,366, including 1,56,756 Dalits, has given a graphic picture of the different types of discriminatory practices in 200 temples.[6]

Many status differences between the Dalits and the upper castes are expressed in terms of ritual purity and pollution. They constantly impinge upon interaction between those who are pure (high castes) and those who are polluted (Dalits for example). Established rules pertaining to purity and pollution makes it necessary for people of different castes to be constantly aware of difference in status. With every drink of water, with every meal and with every contact with the other person, people must ratify social hierarchy of which they are a part and within which every act must be carried out.

Hierarchical structures and attitude between the upper castes and Dalits is thus very much a part of Indian society. It will probably take years, if not decades to remove them.

India, thus, is faced with a contradictory duality. While on the one hand the Indian democratic process is legally removing all legal obstacles against inequality in the caste system, particularly with the parliamentary passage of the prevention of atrocities act in 1989; on the other hand, the hierarchical and discriminatory attitudes within the Hindu system is still very much part of India that it will take decades of education to remove them. The worst victims are the Dalit women. A Seminal study, conducted by the National Campaign for Dalit human rights have enumerated the experience of 500 Dalit women from Andhra Pradesh, Bihar, Tamil

Nadu, Uttar Pradesh has presented a shocking picture of the conditions they live in. The study records the violence physical, sexual and mental.

The Muslim Community

India also has numerously diversified religious, ethnic and linguistic minorities all over the country—minorities that exist since time immemorial.

But the one that is most important are the Muslims, who had a renowned history of their own, and who ruled India for over 700 years before British colonial occupation.

They were a powerful group before the partition of the subcontinent into secular India and Islamic Pakistan; for they constituted 30 per cent of the total population of united India, and had acquired weighty voice in the decisions pertaining to the future of the subcontinent. In fact, they were the ones who insisted on the establishment of a separate Muslim state of Pakistan.

Paradoxically all the Muslim population did not migrate to Pakistan; the ones who stayed back in India constitute 13.4 per cent of the population reaching the high figure of 150 million people, thus making the Muslims the second most populous state nation after Indonesia. The Muslims in India, therefore, were no more as powerful as when the subcontinent was united. In fact they lost their weightiness in Indian politics after the partition of the country.

While the post-independent Indian leadership, centring around Nehru, established constitutionally a secular state for all Indians, the Muslims were looked down upon by most Indian population, who were Hindus, and who remembered their crucial role in the division of the country.

For, it is undeniable that most of the Muslims who stayed back were originally the key supporters for the establishment of Pakistan.

Be that as it may, the important fact is that though they are large in numbers, they have been alienated from Indian politics, and constitute, as a whole, an illiterate and isolated group, heavily mired in deprivation, in impoverishment, and in squalor. They have thus become the most deprived and the most discriminated minority in the country-in fact the new "untouchables"[7]

Muslims, as a whole, are under represented everywhere –in the parliament, in the administrative services, in the armed forces, in the public and private economic sectors. They are mostly in self-employment.

The Indian railways, one of the largest employees in the country has only 4.5 per cent Muslims as employees. And the proportion of Muslim Directors in the private corporate sector is very low. Apart from exceptions, the corporate sector appears to have an unofficial policy of keeping minorities out, especially the Muslims. One survey showed 1 percent of corporate executives are Muslims.

In effect, of this exclusion in the economic sphere there has been the slowing down of the emergence of the middle class.

The high level Sachar Committee, appointed by Prime Minister Singh, has come out with a very damaging report underlining the new fact that Muslims were now worse of than the Dalits.

Committed, as all successive governments have been, to the maintenance of a secular state, there have been concerted attempts to improve their situation. But India has a long way to go so far as Muslims are concerned—even more so than the Dalits. The increasing terrorism of which India is a target from Pakistan have made their situation even more difficult.

The Role of Women

The political panorama is strikingly unprecedented regarding women's empowerment in the political pyramid of Indian politics. India's President, Pratibha Patil, is a women. It is the highest constitutional post in the country—a post that is generally perceived as powerless, but, which, with the long practical experience of the presidency, has acquired considerable informal influence in overcoming difficult political and critical situations. Contemporary history is replete with instances of the President blocking an act or even stopping the nomination of a Prime Ministerial candidate.

The speaker of the Lok Sabha. Meira Kumar, is also a woman. She is a Dalit who was unanimously elected as the head of the lower house of the Parliament. She has not only taken over the position from veteran Marxist leader, Somnath Chaterjee, but will conduct the proceedings of the lower house—undoubtedly a difficult assignment, given the tumultuousness of the house, and the deep political division that dominates the institution. Besides, the speaker occupies a pivotal position in the Indian democratic system. The speaker of the house is undoubtedly a crucial position in so far as years of evolution has given the speaker remarkable powers of monitoring over all the major legislative decisions taken by the Assembly.

Last, but certainly not the least, is Sonia Gandhi, who heads the Congress Party, and who keeps her male colleagues on their toes. Besides, she is the one who nominated Manmohan Singh as the Prime Minister. She had the power to do so and the capacity of making the others—in the corridors of power— to accept such a decision. Sonia Gandhi is the most powerful personage in Indian politics, and it is indeed hardly possible that any major governmental initiative—including the nomination of cabinet ministers can be taken without her agreement.

Interestingly a Chinese observer has characterised the emergence of women in the Indian pyramidal summit as something very significant. "Whether," he wrote, "[8]it is Sonia Gandhi, Pratibha Patil or first Dalit Speaker Meira Kumar, all of them are now controlling men."

But, this remarkable ascendancy at the high institutional level is also visible in other sectors: in professional and administrative fields where women empowerment is equally rampant.

It is true that when one examines the lower and the bottom rungs of the pyramid, one cannot obviously avoid noticing the large quantum of inequality, humiliation and exploitation that characterises the status of women all over the country. It is indeed ubiquitous.

So much has been written on the desperate conditions of ordinary women, all of which is easily accessible, it would be indeed superfluous to repeatedly underline this infelicitous fact, Suffice it to say that their conditions are appalling.

But, what is historically more important are the positive developments that are ratcheting up the status of women. Consider the Government decision to press for a radical new law to reserve for women a third of elected seats in the parliament and the state legislation. Consider the Government's pledge to introduce a bill that will set aside for women half the seats in village councils and city municipalities.

The rise of Indian women as "panchayat leaders is a spectacular achievement" given the fact that India has one of the worst records with respect to the way it treats the female sex.[9]

Consider "microfinance" in the rural areas, principally established to help finance women. More and more Indian entities are recognising the power of micro-finance.

"Micro-finance", wrote an observer, "is not the only answer to solving the poor's problem but it is one good way to help women help themselves. Women self-help groups are burgeoning all across India, and study after study shows that they successfully impact women and bring them out of poverty"[10]

Two Swedish researchers, Ranjula Bali Swain and Fan Yang Wallentin of Uppsala University in Sweden examined the link between microfinance and women's empowerment using household data collected from five states in India in 2000 and 2003. Their results, according to UNDP's *Povery in Focus* "strongly demonstrate" that there is a clear link between women's participation in the Self Help Group and their empowerment.[11]

Here again the role played by the Federal and State Governments to ratchet up the status of women is crucial, and it is more than likely the advancement in this sector is going to be more palpable than with regard to other groups.

VIOLENCE

Notwithstanding the great Gandhian rhetoric favouring non-violence in all public manifestations, India is a violent country replete with all sorts of mob violence, which, declared Subroto Roy, is a "monthly occurance" giving "a lie to our claims of political maturity and democratic development."[12] While this is a universal phenomenon that was rampant in totalitarian societies, and is now often discernible in sports in the West, In India it is everywhere, in all situations and in practically all the circumstances. Argues Roy: "a child is killed by a speeding bus, the driver if he is caught is thrashed to death by a mob of onlookers, and the bus burnt down; a factory closes and workers go on a rampage; or a statute or political personality or religious figure is perceived to have been insulted or desecrated, and crowds take to the streets to burn vehicles or cause mayhem; a process is said to be insulted and rival mobs go to battle with one another,[13]" not to speak of the Indian legislators who frequently "conflate mob behaviour like slogan shouting .... Carrying into the house political methods they have learnt to employ outside it."[14] Or consider the sample of violence that follows a traffic accident by blue line buses in Delhi where not only the guilty bus is routinely burnt, including the passers by who are not spared even though they had no role to play in the accident.

Even in the villages "where peace abounds,"[15] violence against women or dalits can be "even more nauseating than what is" seen in the cities. A quick trip through India's smaller towns—even those untouched by the rapidly changing India would confirm this. Violence is always lurking in the background, and runs through as an undercurrent in Indian society.[16]

India thus is a violent country replete with violence directed against the established state, against minorities, against low caste Hindus, against women, etc.

But communal violence between Hindus and Muslims, is the most fixed and regular feature of Indian behaviour. It was there during the time of the British; and it is there after they had gone, and occurs with greater ferocity, greater regularity and with greater brutality.

Hindu-Muslim collisions have thus blemished the country with some degree of regularity. If anything, they have got worse with the passage of time, and particularly with the emergence of *Hindutva* in the eighties.

This can be attributed to a number of factors. First of all, it was a reaction of many middle class Hindus against what was perceived as bias politics of Nehruvian administration, including some of his successors, in favour of Muslims. While this may be viewed as an exaggeration, it is nonetheless undeniable that such a perception did exist among Hindus, who, on the one hand, admired the Nehruvian leadership for the great goals that it had publicly evoked, but who, on the other hand, upheld the view of the rampancy of bias politics in favour of the Islamic population. This phenomenon of biased perception needs to be seriously examined and objectively analysed—a phenomenon that has generally been ignored.

The second reason pertained to the growth of Islamic fundamentalism in neighbouring Pakistan, and later in Bangladesh. The perception of security threat was widely rampant.

Kashmir also had something to do with the growth of anti-Muslim feeling. Here was, so went the argumentation, the only state with a majority Muslim population which had developed reservations regarding accession to India. In fact, the reservations existed already even during the time of Sheikh Abdullah, who, while known for his secularity, was hesitant regarding Kashmir's accession to India.

Finally there was the absence of any palpable civic ties between Hindus and Muslims. Ashutosh Varshney is probably justified in giving this as one of the valid explanations for Hindu-Muslim enimity.[17]

Without going too much into anecdotal details to advance this argumentation, the author. who was born in Jhelum before the partition, and who had his entire school and partial university education in Lahore, recalls a total absence of any civic interaction between the Hindus and Muslims in the Punjab. Hailing from an upper middle class, educated and sophisticated nationalist family, he does not recall any civic interaction. Interestingly, and notwithstanding the sophistication that governed his family he does not remember even one invitation extended to a Muslim family.

While it is indeed undeniable that second rank right wing Hindu leaders often used the Hindu-Muslim argument for their own advantage, it would be nonetheless too simplistic to base much of the Hindu-Muslim enmity on this argumentation only.

That communal riots are very much a part of Indian life is evident from the important fact that it is at least a yearly occurrence since the independence of the country.[18] While most of them were skimpy, involving few death and few injuries, some of them were gigantically brutal as the one in Ahmedabad in September 1969 causing more than 500 deaths, the other in August 1980 in Moradabad (UP) causing more than 1,500 to 2, 000 deaths, the third in October 1984 resulting in more than 2, 500 deaths, the fourth in December 1992-January 1993 in Bombay where the death figure reached more than 1000, and the one in February 2002 in Gujarat resulting in the death of more than 2000 Muslims.[19]

Most of the communal violence is principally an urban phenomenon, principally occurring in towns that have an important percentage of Muslim population—a population whose political and economic interests clash with those of the Hindus.

While in most of the situations it was a one-sided carnage, principally directed at the Muslim Community, the February 1984 was directed at the Sikhs since Indira Gandhi was assassinated by her Sikh body guards.

Anti-Christian behaviour has also emerged. In June 2009 122 Christians were killed in Orissa where hundreds of houses and churches were destroyed, and from where thousands of them were driven from their villages, and where 3000 were converted to Hinduism.

Violence invariably becomes more intense in the proximity of the election periods, when concerted attempts are usually made to influence the voting behaviour of the population.

Communal violence, thus has become very much a part of Indian political life most of which are specifically directed at the Muslims.

But, there are other types of violence that are increasingly becoming rampant in different parts of India—violence directed at the Dalits, violence by Maoist groups, and violence in north-eastern parts of the country centred around autonomy and independence. The emergence and growth of Maoist rebellion, the formation of CPI (Maoist) in 2004, has also become dimensioned, with violently mutinous group in the country. They are effectively operating in 231 of the 626 districts of the country, and have developed 20,000 armed activists carrying armed forces in a number of areas. Th whole of the northeast region is also known for its massive varigated discontent that continues to maintain its ongoing momentum of defying the Central government and its armed forces. In fact, there are myriad other mutinies all over the country including the one in kashmir.

CORRUPTION

If one were to accept the definition of corruption as "the abusive utilisation of power...for private goal such as personal enrichment or their families (families' friends),"[20] then it is indeed a ubiquitous phenomenon valid for all countries, developed as well as developing. The temptations for seeking material gains by different means is generally perceived as innate. It is inborn among human beings.

Among the developed countries it has evolved; with the passage of time and with the democratisation of the political systems, it has become more restrictive. By no means has it vanished. It is still very much there, for one reads and hears about myriad cases of corruption But, the combination of affluence, the general recognition of ethical standards, and the passage of strict rules of laws against such practices have become dissuasive factors against a very generalised politics of corruption.

In most developed countries laws abound against corruption. In France, for example, the illicit practice of corruption among public servants can lead to a fine of 150,000 euros, and up to 10 years of imprisonment.

Among the developing countries, on the other hand, it is widely rampant: among the poor who need more finances to survive, among the middle classes who have become heavily trapped in the vicious circle of consumerism, and among the rich who have made it into an habit to acquire more and more.

In India it is in all sectors—all over the country. Whether it is a minister at the top, spending a great deal of his time taking a massive amount of kickbacks, or a poor clerk at the bottom of the pyramidal ladder using his minimal power to discreetly place a business file from the bottom of a pile to the top. "It is exercised," confirms A.D. Moddie, "by everybody from *patwari* to Minister. From a ration card to a thousand official clearances to the price of a legislator or a public office, every thing has a price. Even those who mourn a family member's death are not spared harassment for a death certificate. Every control point is regarded as a licence to harass and take increasing sums of money without discretion or principle."[21]

Professor C.J. Daswani has forcefully argued that "today it would seem corruption has not only become more widespread, but it has become more acceptable as a way of life."[22] "Acts of corruption," he has suggested "are transacted overtly, and corrupt people no longer have to hang their heads in shame."[23]

The original nationalist leadership, before independence—deeply influenced by the moral standards established by Gandhi— had developed an impeccable record of austerity.But it is important to note that already in 1937 when Congress ministries were allowed to be established, under the Government of India act of 1935, corruption had surfaced among those who were in power. While the Congress Ministers decided to work on salaries of Rs. 500 per month as against Rs. 2000 they were entitled to; But, within a few weeks it became increasingly evident that corruption had seeped through among those who were involved in governance. Bogus membership of the congress party made its appearance and began to grow. Besides, "there was a scramble for jobs and positions of personal advantage,"[24] So much so that Gandhi told Gandhi Sevak Sangh Workers that "I would go to the length of giving the whole congress organisation a decent burial rather than put up with corruption that is rampant."[25] When independence finally came and congress men settled down to the exercise of power the symptoms seen by Gandhi became even more pronounced.[26] The process of corruption began to systematically take shape in the country.

It would take too long to cover even the important cases of corruption during Nehru-Gandhi period. Suffice it to say that it had become an integral part of the Indian system spread out all over the country. According to Transparency International Index, India ranks 85th from 180 countries' surveyed with a score of 3.4. Since the first iterations of the index India has scored between 2.7 and 3.5, indicating that—despite some progress—corruption continued to be perceived as endemic by different sources.

While corruption is on the increase in all sectors the ones that are most affected are the police force and political corruption. According to 2007 Global Corruption barometer the police has a score of 4.5 on a 5 point scale. The Marketing and Development Research Associations/Transparency India (2006) reports on corruption in trucking operations. The truck drivers pay bribes at every stage of their operations to obtain permits, for traffic violations or toll payments. When transporting goods across the country stoppages by authorities are frequent under the pretext of checking documents. According to the truck drivers, 60 per cent of the checkpoints and forced stoppage are for extorting money.[27]

Political corruption is the second most affected sector. Already in October 1993 N.N. Vohra, made a disquieting report regarding the criminalisation of Indian politics and regarding the nexus among criminals, politicians and bureaucrats. The report highlighted the important fact that criminal network was running virtually a parallel government, and that criminal gangs enjoyed the patronage of all parties. That this was the first hard-hitting report that was written by a man whose credential were meritorious, and who had held high administrative and political positions, including governorship of Kashmir and Jammu State.[28]

Later the situation got even worse. Circumstantial evidence confirms that practices such as buying votes with bribes or promises, or state capture are common in India. In December, 2005, 11 members of Parliament were accused of accepting cash for raising specific questions in the Lok Sabha sessions and subsequently were forced to resign. More recently, a Parliamentary Enquiry Committee was established to look into cash-for votes scam in July 2008. Three Parliamentarians displayed wads of currency notes alleging huge sums of money were offered to them to save the Manmohan Singh Government.

The report presented in December 2008 found the evidence unconvincing and recommended further investigation on the role played by the Parliamentarians.

The entry of criminals into politics—despite laws requiring a public disclosure of candidates' assets, criminal records and educational background—is another alarming facet of political corruption. According to the *Economist* more than a fifth of federal parliamentarians in 2008 faced criminal charges. Of the

522 members in the 2008 parliament 120 were facing criminal charges, around 40 of whom are accused of serious crimes, including murder, and rape.[29]

Another major source of corruption was collection of funds for the parties. The amendment to the Companies Act that originally forbade them from contributing funds to political parties, has opened flood gates to collectors to go about collecting funds.

However, there were nonetheless a series of changes that began to become visible—changes in favour of anti-corruption. Economic liberalisation did have some effect; the power of the bureaucracy declined. Private sector leaders did not have any more to go to the capital to obtain licenses from the bureaucracy to start an industry. What is perhaps even more important is that Prime Minister Manmohan Singh declared that anti-corruption had become top priority of the government.

Committed as all Indian governments have been to disable corruption, concerted efforts were made passing myriad legislation to contain the expansion of this Indian malady. India, perhaps, is one of the few developing countries which has established a well-developed legal and institutional framework to eliminate corruption. The government has indeed received high scores for its legislation. An analysis conducted by Transparency India in 2007 to identify possible gaps between the UN Convention against corruption (UNCAC) and the legal and institutional framework in place in the country. The report confirmed the good quality of the legal framework against corruption in India with the existing legislation compatible with most of the requirements of the UNCAC. The only substantial gap, according to the report, that existed was in the area of whistleblower protection, and obviously in the incapacity of the government to enforce its own legislation.

EDUCATION

The original educational policy, as stipulated in the constitution, required that the government should focus its primary attention on the education of children and adolescents between the ages of 6 and 14. In sum a government focalisation on primary and secondary education.

But the Indian focus was slowly directed on higher education on the ground that it would provide the technical personnel, badly needed by the growing Indian society (doctors, engineers, etc.) and it would generate the necessary acceleration of the urgently needed Indian economic development.

The net result of all this was that there was indeed the establishment of a wide panoply of higher educational institutions. By 2009 India already had 20 central universities, 215 State universities, 100 deemed universities, 5 institutions established (and functioning) under the state, and 13 institutes which were of national importance. Other institutions functioning under these universities and institutions are 16,000 colleges, including 1,800 colleges for women.

In terms of enrolment it has close to 18 million students, making higher education the third largest after China (21 million) and the US (17 million). In terms of the quantum of educational institutions, on the other hand, it tops the world for having as many as 18,000. In terms of public expenditure the Indian performance is equally impressive. 1 per cent of the GDP is devoted to higher education, which is not very low, considering the highest corresponding figure is 1.7 per cent in Finland (the highest in the world), 1.3 per cent in US and 0.8 percent in UK.

Higher education continues to be considered as a major priority since the 11th five year plan (2007-2012) considers its "expansion, inclusion and excellence" as the major objective in the sector of education.

The ramifications of such an expansion can only be advantageous to the country, since there is clearly a close linkage between higher education and rapid economic development. Furthermore the utilisation of the English language for higher education and research has generated considerable advantage of having linguistic access to the research data that is available in the international market. Besides, the English language facilitates Indian student's entry into the educational sector in the western countries. Furthermore, in comparison to many other developed countries it has a long tradition of academic freedom—a freedom that makes it possible to establish a sound basis of quality in higher education.

It is important to note that the higher educational scene has been dominated by private institutions—the vast majority of colleges, that is—and receive grants from the government.

While criticising higher education's shift "from a social institution to industry", observers nonetheless accept the fact "that private higher education has come to stay, and is destined to grow.," since "it will bring competitive merit and force periodical changes in curriculum, pedagogy, examination and governance across the entire educational sector."[30]

In its ongoing efforts to rapidly expand higher education, the India government has taken a major decision in February 2009 of approving the new politics of permitting foreign direct investment in higher education and of freely regulating the entry, operation and the maintenance of foreign educational providers.

This is indeed a landmark development, for India traditionally opposed any importation of foreign educational institutions in India.

While this is compatible with the ongoing Indian opening to the outside world, it has drawn a sharp criticism from many educationists, including Yash Pal, the former Chairman of India's Universities Grants Comission "We don't need foreign universities", he declared, "we need good teachers from abroad who will live here, teach here and (develop) here. Allowing foreign universities in India is a recipe for destroying Indian institutions and turning education into a commodity." Pal feared that, contrary to expectations, the new politics would open floodgates for substandard commercial institutions. For India, in his view, does not have the infrastructure to attract world's top universities like Oxford and Harvard.[31]

But, there are nonetheless, on the other hand, some advantages, of such an opening. For one thing, the influx of international investment may cut India's costs in the sector; for another the enlarged sector of higher education within the country may diminish the quantum of Indian students going outside of India, many of whom, it is known, are lost to India and to Indian economic development since they never return to the country.

There is nonetheless a great deal of argumentation advanced against such an orientation favouring higher education on the ground that India was indeed depriving millions of young Indians from primary and secondary education—an objective that had been clearly stipulated in the constitution. For 40 per cent of the population is still illiterate, and only 15 per cent of the students reach high school.

Since Indian financial and technical manpower resources are still quite limited India will undoubtedly have to face the dilemmic situation of having to choose between basic education and higher education.

The country is faced with proponents of the two schools of thought. While those who give priority to higher education consider that India must continue on this path to maintain the high rate of economic development vital for the prosperity of the country.

Proponents favouring basic education, on the other hand, argue that the normative goal of educating the masses is India's declared objective explicitly stipulated in the Constitution; besides the achievement of such an objective would contribute to the strengthening of democratic institutions.

The new Indian politics of opening the gates to international investments may be the way out of this dilemmic situation, since it would permit the country to devote its own resources more equally to the two sectors.

But, the excessive opening of its higher educational sector to international investments may make India lose national control on higher education.

Should this policy become operational, the only safeguard the government will be left with is the firm establishment of an overarching regulatory policy to keep higher education under control.

References

1. Diana Farrel and Eric Beinhocker, "Next Big Spenders : Indian Middle Class," *Business Week*, 19 May 2007.
2. Ibid.
3. Zoya Hasan. *Politics of Inclusion : Castes, Minorities and Affirmative action*, New Delhi: Oxford University Press, 2009, p. 136.
4. *Le Monde* 25 September 2009.
5. see. Frontline 4 December 2009.
6. Ibid., 31 July 2009.
7. Asra Q Nomani Muslims—India's new 'untouchables', *Los Angeles Times*, 1 December 2006
8. Wu Qiang, "Women calling the shots in male-dominated-Indian politics," *China View*, 6 June 2009.
9. Shoba Narayan, "What is the role of Women in Politics? Growing Stronger," *India Knowledge Wharton, 21 May 2009.*
10. Ibid.
11. UNDP, *Poverty in Focus*, December 2007.
12. Subroto Roy "Mob Violence and Psychology" *Sunday Statesman*, 10 December 2006.
13. Ibid.
14. Ibid.
15. On Mob Violence in India/ Retributions, *http:// retributions.national internet.in /on mob-violence-in india.* Internet 11 August 2009.

16. For details see ibid.
17. Ashutosh, Varshney, *Ethnic Conflict and Civic Life: Hindus and Muslims in India*, Connecticut: Yale University Press, 2002.
18. Brij Lal Gupa, Communal Riots in India Do not Divide the Country, *Instblogs* 19 May 2009, *Internet*.
19. Ibid.
20. Definition of Corruption, *http//www.topie.org/dictionnaire/corruption. Htm,* 15 August 2009.
21. A.D. Moddie, *Leaders of Straw,*New Delhi: HarperCollins Publishers, 1997, p. 106.
22. C.J. Daswani, "Poverty of Commitment", *Yojna,* 26 January 1988.
23. Ibid.
24. Bipin Chandra and Others, *India's Struggle for Independence,* 1988.
25. Ibid.
26. Vohra Report, *Wikipedia the Free Encyclopedia,* 12 June 2009.
27. *http://www.transperanyindia. Org/publication.htm.*
28. Vohra Report, op. cit.
29. *http :www.economist.com/surveys/displaystory-cfm?story id-12749771.*
30. Pawan Agarwal, *Indian Higher Education: Envisioning the Future,* New Delhi: Sage Publications, 2009.
31. M. Shreelata "India's Higher Education Bill Criticised", 21 July 2009, *Science and Development Network, internet* 23 August 2009.

7

Leadership: A Growing Decline

Leadership is influence—nothing more, nothing else

James C. Maxwell 2007

Without going into the different definitions of leadership—for there are indeed numerous with different orientations and different ostentations—suffice it to say that while living together as a societal group, which is arguably the case with all societies, one is invariably faced with the phenomenon of leaders and leadership; for visions have to be conceived, actions have to be taken, decisions have to be made and members of the society have to be mobilised to a common cause and to a common objective.

To successfully reach these goals, the leader as Sun Tzu, the Chinese thinker of the sixteenth century had aptly argued, must possess, cumulatively, the following characteristics: trustworthiness, intelligence, courage and discipline, for "reliance on intelligence alone results in rebelliousness. Exercise of humaneness alone results in weakness. Fixation on trust results in folly. Dependence on the strength of courage results in violence, Excessive discipline and sternness in command result in cruelty."[1] Whereas, elaborated Sun, "when one has all the five virtues together, each appropriate to its function, then one can be a leader."[2]

The other aspect that needs to be elaborated upon is the function of the leadership. What would be the broad framework of its activities? And how can it be defined ?

Here too elaboration was problematic. Myriad definitions abound. For the sociologist, Peter Drucker, "the only definition of a leader is someone who has followers;" for John C. Maxwell "leadership is influence—nothing more, nothing less," whereas for Warren Bennis "leadership is a function of knowing yourself, having a vision that is well-communicated, building trust among colleagues, and taking effective action to realise your own leadership potential."[3]

But, the one that seemed most realistic, and most practical was that of Gary Cohen. For him the leader must set direction and must possess the real quality to put "the right people in right positions, seek insights from all levels, and ensure resources are all allocated to the highest priority while acting ethically at all times and engaging people to stretch beyond what is comfortable, to maximise results."[4]

While leadership is as old as history, our focus begins with Indian nationalism in the early 20th century when India was organising and gearing itself into a movement for independence during colonial rule.

Originally the leaders, who were cautious and moderate, looked up to the British, and worked for the eventual establishment of an Indian political system that was modelled after the British system of governance—consensually perceived as superior to anything that existed anywhere in the world at the time. The swath of the earlier nationalist leaders like Ferozeshah Mehta, Gopal Krishna Gokhale, Dadabhai Naroji, and M.G. Ranade, whose power base was amongst the Bombay intelligentsia, and whose principal objective, was to ratchet up mild pressures on the colonial power to introduce reforms that would ensure greater Indian representation at the political and the administrative levels. They were the ones who operated comfortably with the British, and they were the ones who listened to the advise of the British rulers of "hastening slowly" in their actions for reforms. While they were indeed successful in persuading the British to undertake a pacific process of reforms, the realm of their political activities were generally perceived as too moderate and too functional in a rapidly changing India.

With the rapid movement of national and international events, most of which were changing the political panorama of the country and the world, including the brutal British massacre of unarmed Indians in Amritsar killing 379, and injuring 1200 (known as Jallianwala Bagh or Amritsar massacre) on 13 April 1919 by Brigadier Reginald Dryer's troops, and the emergence of Bolshevik Russian Revolution of 7th

November 1917 (in defiance of the capitalist system), there emerged in India a militant leadership that favoured a more outgoing and more active defiance of the British. While there were quite a few militant leaders, the most important were the Marathi leader Bal Gangadhar Tilak, and the Punjabi Leader Lala Lajpat Rai. The one (Tilak) experimented with mass focus appeals and even some violence that resulted in his imprisonment, and the other, (Lajpat Rai) died of injuries on 17 November 1928 in a black flag demonstration that he had organised against John Simon on 30 October 1928 who was heading a StatutoryCommission appointed by the British Government.

While these movements did have a great impact on nationalism, making it more militant, more violent and more openly defiant of the British, they were nonetheless regional in character lacking the national dimension.

New Nationalism under Gandhi

It was, however, the emergence of Mohandas Karamchand Gandhi in Indian politics that transformed the very nature and pattern of nationalist struggle, and projected a new concept of leadership whose basic objective was to strive for the real independence of India.

Having acquired considerable militant experience in South Africa against apartheid through a massive and bold strategy of political struggle that was pacific, non-violent and self-inflicting, he took the same type of action when he entered political life in India.

All of this was very different from what India was experiencing before, and all of this was recognisable by the mass of Indians as a part of their lives for which they were prepared to follow Gandhi. Consider Gandhi's famous decision to personally walk to the sea to extract sea salt as a protest against the British decision to impose tax on salt. He was not alone to do so, for there were indeed thousands who followed him to do the same.

Without going into all the details of his political life—for much has already been written about him—suffice it to say that basing himself on definitions of leadership proposed here, Gandhi (a) had transformed the Indian National Congress into a mass movement of people from all levels—from the top to the bottom; (b) had collected around himself a group of leaders who had consensually accepted his leadership; (c) had proclaimed, through the years, his goal of liberating India; and (d) had completely confused the British regarding how they should handle him since much of his political actions were very different from what they were used to.

In effect, Gandhi was a "charismatic" leader. While it would be impossible to apply all the characteristics of charisma, as defined by the German sociologist, Max Weber, since the periods, environment and history are different of Europe and India, the broad framework is general enough to apply his broad definition to Gandhi. For Weber, a charismatic leader must possess "certain quality of an individual personality by virtue of which he is set apart from ordinary men and treated as endowed with supernatural and superhuman, or at least specifically exceptional powers or qualities."[5]

While Gandhi fitted well into the general framework of leadership, as proposed in this study, there were nonetheless specific Indian dimensions connected with his personality.

First of all he radically transformed the way he dressed himself. It was very similar to the one attired by the rural poor. Though Churchill maliciously described him as "the half-naked Faqir," his new attire had a perspicuous effect on the ordinary people of India with whom he instantly struck a chord who thought that he was one of them. While many Westerners mocked at his attire, the oriental attitude was different. Like the one of the Egyptian correspondent of *Al-Ahram* who interviewed him at Port Said when Gandhi was on his way to attend the Round Table Conference in London. He was struck by the humbleness of his attire and described it in the following picturesque manner: "bareheaded, naked above the waist, wrapped in a white cotton loincloth from which hung a metal chain connected to a watch with a phosphorescent dial, which could not have cost more than a few piastres."[6]

To detect a national leader with a demeanour like theirs—which was not the case with his nationalist predecessors—broke down the psychological barrier that invariably estranged them from the preceding affluent middle class leaders based essentially in urban areas. That this must have been an important factor in invigorating his leadership among the people is evident from the rapidity with which people turned to him.

Gandhi's religiosity also had considerable impact in the enhancement of his leadership. Like most people in India he was an exceedingly a religious person who derived considerable inspiration from the Gita and Mahabharta, and who combined religiosity with politics, a combination that made it possible for him to dialogue and build bridges with ordinary people. But, Gandhi, at the same time, was a very secular person who made it a point to invoke different religions is his daily prayer meetings. However, while secular, he would invariably cite from his own religious texts—texts he was most familiar with and the ones which had influenced his life. "I find solace," he wrote "in the Bhagvad Gita that I miss in the Sermon on the Mount. When disappointment stares me in the face and all alone I see not one way of light, I go back to the Bhagvad Gita. I find a verse here and there, and I immediately begin to smile in the midst of overwhelming tragedies—and my life is full of external tragedies—and if they left no visible or indelible scar on me, I owe it all to the teaching of Bhagavad-Gita."[7]

The third aspect of Gandhi's leadership was that it was action oriented. Whatever he wanted his followers to do, he did it himself first before calling upon the others to follow him. His entire political life was devoted on setting an example. To express his political dissatisfaction at the British imposition of tax on salt he decided to walk to the sea to make salt himself, followed by a mass of people to do the same, and even selling it in the market. When the Indian leader called upon the people to boycott English textile, he set the example of using the spinning wheel to make his own clothes. This pattern of activity was a great mobilisation factor.

There was then the whole system of fasts he carried out periodically, the objective of which was to restrain actions or to force authorities to take a certain action. In all Gandhi fasted 17 times. The results were indeed striking. Consider his decision to fast until death in Calcutta to stop Muslim/Hindu riots, which the authorities were unable to stop, But his decision to do so finally led to the stoppage of riots. The impact of fast was so great that it led Louis Fischer to declare that when "Gandhi fasts, the Empire trembles".

While a number of strategic factors resulted in the transfer of power, Gandhi's role was crucial. He shall, therefore, go down in history as one of the ratcheting pressures upon the British.

Post-Gandhi Leadership

But, Gandhi's role after independence obviously became less important. What was then needed was a new type of leadership for the governance and modernisation of the country. While the Indian leader did have views on modernisation, they were generally perceived as inconsequential to the 20th century India.

In any event, Gandhi' was no more, having been assassinated a couple of years after independence by a Hindu fanatic. His thinking had become a closed book.

In any event, even if he had been alive, he would have been no more relevant, since the great and charismatic Gandhian leadership had focussed solely on the Indian nationalist movement; whereas what was needed after independence were votaries interested in the general and rather a vague goal of post-independent modernisation of the country.

The mantle of leadership, thus, had to fall on a different type of personality—a personality with a different vision—a vision of governance and development. The new task fell upon Nehru. In fact, Gandhi had already named him as his successor much before the independence of the country.

But, even at this point of time, many Indians still continue to wonder the reasons that led Gandhi to choose Nehru; for the latter had, through his innumerable writings, proposed a highly westernised socio-economic system that was clearly incompatible with what Gandhi had in mind regarding the future of India.

Sardar Patel was the other possible successor. Since many considered him, at the time, as a gigantic organiser, and non-ideologically oriented, practical, assertive politician; many considered him as the most appropriate personality for leading and governing India immediately after independence.

In any event, the mantle of leadership fell upon Nehru as the Prime Minister of India. After Gandhi, he was the most popular, visible and loved leader, who went around the country loudly reflecting about the future of India—much more than any of his colleagues. He inspired devotion and trust. But, hardly anyone among those who happen to be at the bottom of the hierarchical ladder were familiar with his socio-economic ideas. It is one of the great paradoxes of India that, more often than not, a massive devotion to a leader is not linked to any rational reasons, but is underpinned by some form of emotionalism, verging on to religiosity. Think of the emotional spectacle of a mass of Indians sitting on the floor with folded hands, in front of a leader almost representing god. This may not be any more the case today, since rampant bitterness has surged among even rural Indians, but this was indeed a traditional cultural behaviour among many Indians when India had any iconic leadership during the nationalist movement. Think of the satisfaction that many Indians had of visibly seeing a luminary. It was almost a spiritual experience, which the Hindus call *darshan.*

In any event Nehru was one of those icons. Here was a man, sophisticated, aristocratic, rich, etc., who considered himself almost half-English, who was indeed loved by rural India. Like Gandhi, he possessed a charisma, as Max Weber would put it, endowed with exceptional powers and qualities not accessible to ordinary people.

But Nehru was different from Gandhi in terms of leadership even though he was charismatic. While possessing the qualities of "passion, responsibility and proportion," he did not have the same decisiveness as Gandhi. For possessed with known Hamletian instinct, he often debated within himself as to what he should do, and often wondered if he had taken the right action. While these are nonetheless meritorious qualities that we all should possess, it is arguable if such thinking would not pre-dispose a leader to inactivity in the middle of an action. Furthermore, unlike Gandhi, he was not surrounded only by devoted people, but had to confront the new phenomenon of the struggle for power, and had to face dissension regarding the political-economic-social road India should travel

The situational factors, additionally, were no more the same. India was no more struggling for its independence from the British. The British had gone, and Nehru's party had acquired the power of running the country and had to give a specific direction regarding the road it should travel.

His charismatic leadership, and his political determination had resulted in the expansion of the democratic institutions India had inherited from the colonial rule. With the establishment of a liberal constitution, and with the staging of free electoral consultation, he had irremediably made India opt for the democratic path. Also, he pushed the country to opt for a socio-economic regime whose underpinnings were socialistic, even though vague. For all this Nehru's leadership would be remembered.

But, charismatic leadership, as defined earlier, has become, with a movement of time, a rare quality among Indian political leaders. To risk a generalisation, one could argue that none of the successive Prime Ministers fell into the category of charismatic leadership. They were of course all leaders since they were heading governments, and since all of them, according to Peter Drucker, had followers, or according to James C. Maxwell were equipped with a great deal of influence. There was Indira Gandhi who took a great deal of landmark actions like winning a war against Bangladesh or like launching a nuclear test in defiance of the international community. There was Narasimha Rao who made the major economic turnaround in the early nineties, There was Girija Shankar Vajpayee who initiated powerful actions including pushing India to become a nuclear power. And, there was Manmohan Singh who inaugurated a process of good relations with the United States.

Thus all of them were leaders, as defined in the traditional sense, but none of them reached the charismatic stage.

In fact, if one examines the performance of the swath of Prime Ministers that India had had, one could risk a generalisation, by arguing that there has been a slow but nonetheless secular decline in political leadership after Gandhi and Nehru. This has become a continuous process and continues to head downwards.

One of the most important signs of this secular decline is the emergence of moral turpitude among the leaders. This may or may not be the case, but there is undoubtedly a remarkable consensus within the population of this state of affairs. There appears to exist an obsessive search for power. This is a universal phenomenon present everywhere, but in India it has reached the outer limits. It is a part of cultural behaviour at all levels of the hierarchy

However, in addition to the wide prevalence of such a perception, the Indian public opinion has generally come to the conclusion of the existence of rampant corruption at the political level. Gone indeed are the days of Gandhi and Nehru of living in austerity and simply. Indian politics is strongly characterised by a blind search for power and inscrutable attraction for material gain.

By no means is it being suggested that every politician on the national scene was power hungry and preoccupied with material gain. There are indeed many meritorious examples of impeccable good behaviour. But it has nonetheless penetrated the system and cannot really be eradicated.

The decline in the leadership is also due to a number of changing situational factors.

The first clearly is the emergence of coalition politics in the Indian system. Gone indeed are the days of the earlier period when a majority party rule was the order of the day, when a level of stability was rampant in governance and when similarity of ideological views was common. But, Coalition politics has become a part of the Indian system after the Nehru-Gandhi period, the net result of which is that the majority party has to invariably negotiate with small regional parties in order to establish a comfortable majority to govern. That, this is by no means an easy procedure, for it involves a long and arduous negotiations. The power of the Prime Minister certainly undergoes a decline since he has to appease a number of similar parties to establish a government. And when the government is established, the Prime Minister is clearly aware of the fact that his own decision making power has been clearly restrained since he has to consult other parties in the government before a decision can be taken. This was the constant refrain of all the prime ministers the author has interviewed. One of them had, in fact, appreciated the working of the system since it made it possible for him to survive lengthily.

There are some who are prepared to argue that the "coalition governments are effective in enhancing democratic legitimacy, representativeness and national unity,"[8] and that major policy shifts like neo-liberal economic reforms, federal decentralising, and grass roots decentralisation were only possible with the coalition governments.

While this argumentation may have some creditability, the slowness of the decision making process, compounded with growing instability, generated by the coalition government, outweigh the advantages of such a formation. For India can hardly afford any political instability or a any haphazard decision making process in the 21st century, not to speak of the declination of power of the Prime Minister.

Another major modification is the growing separation of political power between the ones who are holding it and those who have been installed in formal governmental positions. The latest example is that of Manmohan Singh who was an economist by reputation and who is. not the holder of real decisional power on a wide array of subjects. It is difficult to imagine that Prime Minister Singh would be able to conduct important political decisions without the prior approval of Sonia Gandhi who was the real power holder. This is by no means an isolated incident since practically all the prime ministers after the Nehru Gandhi era, found themselves in such a position.

The third important phenomenon was the emergence of the States as the important holders of power at the regional level, thus making it difficult, if not impossible, for the PM to go ahead with his policies without taking into account the views of the regional leaders.

The economic turnaround in the 90s also resulted in the diminution of political power at the centre, for the first time in India's post-independent history the emergence of economic leadership from the private economic sector—a leadership which was much less restrained in designing policies in the economic sector. Years after the economic turnaround, the political leadership,while formally maintaining power, had to abandon large sectors of economic decisions to the private economic sector.

Having accepted the politics of liberalisation, the political leadership could not possibly decide on the economic sector without the implicit or explicit approval of the leaders of the Indian industries.

Connected with the economic turnaround, there was also a decline in the power of the bureaucratic leadership—a leadership that had literally ruled India for so many years since independence.

While the broad framework of the Indian economic orientations were still decided by the Indian political leadership—now in close consultation with economic leaders— the power of the bureaucracy had declined in so far as the economic entrepreneur did not have to go to Delhi, the capital of India, for obtaining the so-called licences or permits to expand in the economic sector They could now work on their own, without having to plead with the bureaucracy to expand in the economic sector.

Another factor that restrained the power of the Indian leaders was the growing globalisation of the Indian economy. They had to take into account the views of the other governments and face the pressures of other powers.

The power of the political leadership had thus declined through the years. It was no more completely sovereign in all its decisions since it has to take into account (1) the political power residing outside the governmental authority, (2) to listen to the coalition partners, (3) take into account the views and pressures of the economic leaders, and the pressures emanating from the international system, and (4) have to accept the regional leaders who had become powerful factors in state and central politics.

One wonders if this declination of political leadership is not the result of the evolution of the whole system— system that does not any more needs an outstanding and charismatic leadership of the years gone by but leaders who operate in cooperation with other forces—including the ones in the economic, social, technological and international sectors.

References

1. Leslie Pockell with Adrine Avila (edited), *The 100 Greatest leadership Principles of all Time* (New York : Warner Books, 2007, p. 35.
2. *Ibid.*
3. Our Definition of Leadership, *http :www. teal,org. uk/ leadership/definition.htm*
4. Gary Cohen, Defining Leadership, *Leadership Excellence. Internet,* August 2000.
5. Max Weber, *Theory of Social and Economic Organisation,* New York: Free Press. 1947, pp. 358-359.
6. "Gandh in Egypt"*http://weekly.ahram.org.eg/print/2002/ 617/chrnels.htm.*
7. see, Jyotsna Kamat, Mahatma Gandhi Album : Gandhi on Bhagavad Gita. "*Http://www. Kamat. Com/mmgandhi/ mkggita. htm.*
8. Mahendra Prasad Singh and Anil Mishra, *Coalition Politics in India : Problems and Prospects,* New Delhi : Manohar, 2005.

Summing Up

The greatest landmark in India's mottled history, under examination in this treatise, is the legacy of *political democracy*—a legacy of which India has become a consistent champion. With the exception of the two years of dark period of Indira Gandhi's authoritarianism, the country has faithfully followed and developed democratic institutions in the country.

This should not have been the case since there is a general belief that democracy can successfully operate only in a country that was economically advanced, materially prosperous and politically stable.

India could hardly fit into this category since it was economically underdeveloped, materially impecunious, and politically mired in myriad revolts, oppositions, mutinies, etc.

Yet, notwithstanding the absence of all these prerequisite qualities, India has indeed gone the democratic way, for there are, in George Kennan's opinion, others factors which are equally important—factors that comes from "day-to-experience with the modalities of self-government...from experience, from long encounter with reality" and "from the quality of habit."[1]

Having acquired limited "day-to-day experience with the modality of self government," compounded with "the quality of habit" under the Empire, India was consensually able to continue on the democratic path after independence.

The whole system, furthermore, was reinforced by the important fact that the iconic nationalist leadership, represented by Gandhi, Nehru, Patel, Azad, etc., were fervent advocates of the system.

One wonders if Hinduism, with its high level of abstraction, tolerance and pluralistic mind-set was not an important contributory factor to the reinforcement of this process. Besides, there was nothing else to which the Indians could turn to; for there was a broad consensual agreement in the Indian leadership that there was nothing else that could constitute as a viable substitute—since the Indians were already beholden to the benefits they had experienced—though very limited—of the system during the time of the empire.

It was the combination of all these factors that may have generated this attraction to political pluralism in India.

The Indian leaders, though never enamoured by Winston Churchill, given his unsavoury record on Indian independence, could not have possibly ignored his relevant Churchillian expressions on democracy. "No one pretends," he declared, "that democracy is perfect or all-wise, it has been said that democracy is the worst form of government except all those other forms that have been tried from time to time.[2]"

Unlike India's consistent faith in political democracy, its economic options, on the other hand, were not that consistent. They were mutated in the course of India's economic evolution. The Nehruvian—Gandhian years were dominated by the economic options Nehru had taken at the time of the Indian independence: the options of the centrality of the State, of the primordiality of heavy industrial growth, of the focalisation on making India economically independent through minimal economic interaction with the outside world.

The record was not that impressive. While India did finally grow into a developing industrial nation, the economic day-to-day lives of the people, on the other hand, continued to stagnate. The people were really not better off.

The power of democracy finally prevailed in the early nineties of the 20th century, since India decided to take another economic option—the option of introducing liberal economy, of opening up economically to the outside world, of maximising exports, of attracting foreign investments. In sum, moving on—though prudently—to some form of economic globalisation.

The final visible effect of the new turnaround was indeed striking. While the country was still dismally poor, a new level of prosperity did surface with a high level of annual growth (8 per cent), with a burgeoning middle class, with lower illiteracy rate, with greater economic integration with the planet, etc.

Its international image began to show signs of improving, with the manifestation of greater interest in its actions among the international actors. Along with China, India is now perceived as a growing nation with a glass half- full, rather than half-empty.

There has thus been a remarkable mutation in all these sixty years of independence; and if it continues to grow visibly in the years to come, the future projections may be even more decisive, even more bullish and even more ubiquitous in improving the lives of people.

Without fuelling a rancorous debate at the end of this treatise, one wonders if this visible up-gradation is not the cumulative result of the initial Nehruvian option to give India a sound industrial base, and the new economic option of opening up increasingly to the outside world.

References

1. George F. Kennan, op. cit., p. 176.
2. Angela Partington, *The Oxford Dictionary of Quotations*, Oxford: Oxford University Press, 1990, p. 202.

Bibliography

BASIC LITERATURE

1. BOOKS AND DOCUMENTS

Aiyar, S.P. and R.Sirinivasan (edited) *Studies in Indian Democracy,* Bombay: Allied Publishers Private Limited, 1965.

Ali, Mohammad, *My Life: A Fragment,* Lahore: SH Mohammad Ashraf, 1966.

Antonova, K., G. Bongard/Levin/G. Kotovsky, *A History of India*, Moscow: Progress Publishers, 1979, in two books.

Bahaduri, Amit, & Deepak Nayyar, *The Intelligent Person's Guide to Liberalisation* New Delhi: Penguin Books, 1996.

Barraclough, G., *Introduction to Contemporary History,* London: Penguin Books, 1966.

Carr, E.H., *What is History*, London: Penguin Books, 1988.

Chadda, Maya, *Building Democracy in South Asia, India, Nepal Pakistan,* New Delhi: Vistaar Publication, 2000.

Chaudhuri, Nirad C., *Thy Hand Great Anarch: India: 1821-1952,* London: Chatto & Windus, 1988.

Crystal, David (edited), *Penguin Encyclopedia,* London: Penguin Books, 2004.

Durbin, E.F.M., *The Politics of Democratic Socialism,* London: Routledge, 1945.

Gandhi, M.K., *India of my Dreams,* Ahmedabad: Navjivan Publishing House, 1940.

Gandhi, Sonia, *edited by Two Alone, Two Together: Letters Between Indira Gandhi and Jawaharlal Nehru,1922-1964* New Delhi, Penguin Books, 2004.

Giddens, Anthony, *The Third Way: The Renewal of Social Democracy,* Cambridge: Plity Press, 1999.

Guha, Ramchandra, *India After Gandhi: The History of the World's Largest Democracy,* London: Macmillan, 2007.

Hasan, Zoya, *Politics of Inclusion: Castes, Minorities and Affirmative Action,* New Delhi: Oxford University Press, 2009.

Hayat. Sikander, *The Charismatic Leaders: Quaid-i-Azam Mohammad Ali Jinnah and the Creation of Pakistan,* Karachi: Oxford University Press, 2008.

James, Lawrence, *Raj: The Making of British India,* London: Abacus, 1997.

Kapur, Harish, Foreign Policies of India's Prime Ministers, Lancer: New Delhi: Frankfort 11, 2009.

Keay, John, *India: A History,* London: The Folio Society, 2003, 2 volumes.

—— *The Honourable Company: History of the English East India Company,* New Delhi: HarperCollins Publisher, 1991.

Kennan, George F., *At a Century's Ending: Reflections 1982-1995,* London: W.W. Norton and Company, 1966.

Krishnamurthy, T.S., *The Miracle of Democracy: India's Amazing Journey,* New Delhi: HarperCollins Publishers India, 2008.

Lippmann, Walter, *The Public Philosphy,* New York: Little Brown, 1955.

Macmillan, Margaret, *Dangerous Games: The Uses and Abuses of History,* New York: The Modern Library, 2008.

Marx, K. & F. Engels, *On Colonialism,* Moscow; Foreign Languages Publishing House, 1960.

Mason, Philip, *The Men Who Ruled India*, London: Pan Books Limited, 1987.

Mirza, Hamayun, *From Plassey to Pakistan,* Washington DC: United Press of America Inc, 2001.

Moddie, A.D., *Leaders of Straw: India's First 50 Years,* New Delhi: HarperCollins Publisher, 1977.

Moss, Robert, *The Collapse of Democracy,* London: Abacus, 1977.

Nayyar, Deepak, *Liberalization and Development,* New Delhi: Oxford University Press, 2008.

Nehru, Jawaharlal, *Toward Freedom: An Autobiography of Jawaharlal Nehru,* New York: John Day, 1942.

Patnaik, Utsa, *The Republic of Hunger and Other Essays,* Gurgaon: Three Essays Collective, 2008.

Royle, Trevor, *The Last Days of the Raj*, London: Coronet Books, 1984.

Sahai, Shashi B., *The Politics of Corruption: The Goddess that Failed,* New Delhi: Gyan Publishing House, 1995.

Sarila, Narendra Singh, *The Shadow of the Great Game: The Untold Story of India's Partition,* New Delhi: Harper Collins Publisher India, 2008.

Singh, Jaswant, *Jinnah India-Partition Independence,* New Delhi: Rupa, 2009.

Singh, Pahendra Prasad and Anil Mishra, *Coalition Politics in India:Problems and Prospects,* New Delhi: Manohar 2005.

Subramanium, T.S.R., *Journeys Through Babudom and Netaland: Governance in India,* New Delhi: Rupa and Co, 2004.

Trevelyan, G.O., *The Life and Letters of Lord Macaulay,* Middlesex : Echo Library 1876.

Varshney, Asutosh, *Ethnic Conflict and Civic Life: Hindus and Muslims in India*, Connecticut: Yale University Press, 2002.

Weber, Max, *Theory of Social and Economic Organisation,* New York: Free Press, 1947.

Wild, Antony, *The East India Company—Trade and Conquest from 1600,* London: Harper Collins, 1999.

Williams, Hywell, *Cassell's Chronology of World History: Dates, Events and Ideas that made History* London: Weidenfeld and Nicolson, 2005.

2. ARTICLES

Chandhoke, Neera, "Participation, Representation and Democracy in Contemporary India," *American Behavioral Scientist,* Volume 52, No 6, 2009.

Cohen, Gary, "Defining Leadership," *Leadership Excellence, Internet* August 2000.

Jain, Purnendra, "Japan to Shift Aid Focus from China to India," *Asia Times, 11 March 2004.*

Katju, Markandey, "Look Back on the Caste System," *New Age Weekly,* 1-7 February 2009.

Kristianasen, Wendy, "Plongée au Coeur de L'Inde Musulmane," *Le Mone Diplomatique* January 2009.

Lewis, John K, " Some Consequences of Giantism," *World Politics,* April 1991.

Noorani, A.G., "Cripps and India's Partition," *Frontline,* 2 August 2002.

Sutherland, Jabez T., "The New Nationalist Movement in India," *The Atlantic,* October 1908.

Index

D

J

N